MY STREET FOOD KITCHEN

To my boys: Patrick, Liam and Riley

MY
STREET
FOOD
KITCHEN

JENNIFER JOYCE

PHOTOGRAPHY JEAN CAZALS

MURDOCH BOOKS

CONTENTS

INTRODUCTION

Taking an overseas holiday is one of life's greatest pleasures. What's not to like about being transported to an exotic destination, with no schedule to stick to, experiencing life at your own pace? Travel feeds the soul, but more importantly it satisfies curious and voracious appetites.

How better to immerse oneself in the culture of a place than to eat on the street among the locals? Eating the genuine versions of dishes I thought I knew; discovering an unknown ingredient: it never fails to delight me. Along with each new taste, the surrounding noises and smells stay forever in my mind: the corn tortillas in Mexico, freshly pressed and eaten hot from the griddle; caramel-glazed pork grilled over the tiniest of charcoal braziers in Hanoi; a tantalising slurp of Japanese yuzu juice; or the crunch of a tamarind-spiked bhel puri on a Mumbai beach. Wondrous food discoveries continually shape my cooking and the good news is that this delicious education never ends.

Street food is immediate, vibrant and not necessarily subtle. It thrills us with its crunch, spice, sweetness, saltiness or sour tang. I wanted to pull together these punchy flavours and recipes for the home cook. *My Street Food Kitchen* is the result of decades of travel to twenty-four countries across all parts of the globe. This isn't just dishes from roadside stalls and markets but food from the heart and soul of each region, plus fresh salads, sides and sweets. Returning home to real life is the hard part after a great adventure, but the best way to recapture your memories is to fill your house with the aromas and tastes of your travels.

Street food can sometimes be hard to decipher, with too many ingredients and laborious preparation, so I've created healthier and more delicious renditions without compromising authenticity. More than two years of work has gone into developing, testing and retesting these recipes so they are foolproof. And if you can squeeze another piece of equipment (or three) into your kitchen there is much to gain from the use of crockpots, pressure cookers and electric mixers that will make your cooking faster and easier.

This kind of food was meant for sharing so, if you want to treat your friends to a crazy good feast, 'Get ahead' tips are included with each recipe. The portions are generous and most recipes serve four to six people, so no one will go hungry. ENJOY!

JENNIFER

NEW AMERICAN FOOD

DIRTY BURGERS & CRUNCHY KALESLAW

Buffalo chicken wings are a national treasure in America and happy hour wouldn't be the same without them. Their deeply messy and addictive charms are hard to resist, but they don't have to be deep-fried and drowned in spicy butter: they're every bit as good roasted with a home-made hot sauce. The type of pepper sauce you use makes a big difference; I prefer one with a fruity taste that's not too blow-your-head-off spicy.

BAKED STICKY BUFFALO CHICKEN WINGS WITH CELERY STICKS & BLUE CHEESE DIP

PREPARATION: 20 MINUTES, PLUS OVERNIGHT MARINATING • COOKING: 1 HOUR • SERVES: 4–6 AS A SNACK

3 garlic cloves, finely chopped

1½ tablespoons olive oil

1½ tablespoons apple cider vinegar

3 teaspoons paprika

3 teaspoons Worcestershire sauce

1 teaspoon celery salt

80 ml (2½ fl oz/⅓ cup) Frank's® Redhot® sauce or other spicy cayenne pepper sauce

90 g (3¼ oz/¼ cup) honey

1 kg (2 lb 4 oz) chicken wings, halved at the joint

Celery sticks with blue cheese dip

150 ml (5 fl oz) sour cream or crème fraîche

60 ml (2 fl oz/¼ cup) mayonnaise

75 g (2¾ oz) blue cheese (Danish or roquefort), crumbled

1 teaspoon white wine vinegar

Worcestershire sauce

4 celery stalks, cut into batons

Combine all of the ingredients except the chicken wings in a large bowl and stir well. Season with freshly ground black pepper. Add the chicken wings, toss to coat, then cover and refrigerate for 24 hours or overnight.

Preheat the oven to 210°C (415°F) or 190°C (375°F) fan forced.

Drain and reserve the marinade. Spread the chicken wings on a very large baking tray and bake for 30 minutes. Remove from the oven, pour off the excess oil, then add the reserved marinade and toss to coat well. Increase the oven temperature to 230°C (450°F) or 210°C (415°F) fan forced and cook for another 30 minutes, tossing a couple of times during cooking to coat in the glaze. The wings should be sticky and glazed with most of the marinade evaporated. Serve on a large platter with finger bowls of warm water for washing sticky fingers.

CELERY STICKS WITH BLUE CHEESE DIP

Combine the sour cream, mayonnaise, blue cheese, vinegar and a splash of Worcestershire sauce in a bowl. Season to taste with salt and freshly ground black pepper, then pour into a serving bowl. Arrange the celery sticks in cups for dipping.

GET AHEAD You can marinate the wings overnight and cook the first 30 minutes on the morning of serving. Roast for the final 30 minutes just before serving. The blue cheese and celery can be prepared the day before and refrigerated. Cover the celery with cold water to keep it crisp.

No, this isn't a remedy for cleaning out your refrigerator, but a supersized chopped antipasto salad that was first created in Chicago. Chunks of juicy iceberg lettuce, diced veggies, cubes of salty cheese, salami and pickled peppers are tossed in a red wine and oregano vinaigrette that's galactically good.

GARBAGE SALAD

PREPARATION: 20 MINUTES • SERVES: 4–6

½ iceberg lettuce
¼ radicchio
1 small red onion
150 g (5½ oz) cherry tomatoes
1 yellow capsicum (pepper)
1 small celery heart
5 radishes
10 slices Italian salami
90 g (3¼ oz) asiago, gouda or
   provolone cheese
2 slices sourdough bread, toasted
10 pepperoncini (pickled Tuscan
   peppers)
15 small basil leaves

Red wine vinaigrette
50 ml (1¾ fl oz) red wine vinegar
1 teaspoon dried oregano
60 ml (2 fl oz/¼ cup) sunflower oil
3 teaspoons caster (superfine) sugar
3 teaspoons dijon mustard
½ garlic clove, crushed

To make the vinaigrette, put all of the ingredients into a glass jar with a fitted lid. Season with salt and freshly ground black pepper. Shake well and set aside.

Wash the lettuce and radicchio and discard the outer leaves. Coarsely chop the leaves. Finely chop the red onion. Halve the cherry tomatoes. Quarter the yellow capsicum, discard the seeds and membrane, and cut it into 1 cm (⅜ inch) pieces. Thinly slice the celery heart and radishes.

Cut the slices of salami into small strips. Cut the cheese into 1 cm (⅜ inch) cubes. Cut the sourdough toast into 1 cm (⅜ inch) cubes. Chop the pepperoncini into 1 cm (⅜ inch) slices.

Put all of the salad ingredients in a large bowl. Pour the dressing over and toss to coat. Serve immediately.

GET AHEAD The dressing, salad and croutons can all be prepared earlier in the day, then stored in separate containers, covered and refrigerated. Dress just before serving.

Celeriac is a vegetable that's often overlooked, but don't underestimate its appeal. It makes killer mash or can be julienned raw in salads. The gnarly root of a type of celery plant, it retains that 'celery' taste but with the crisp bite of raw carrot. Its texture is key in this composite of veggies tossed in a sharp lemon and poppyseed vinaigrette. Perfect served with ribs, steaks or fried chicken.

CELERIAC SLAW WITH APPLE, HAZELNUTS & POPPYSEED DRESSING

PREP: 20 MINUTES • COOKING: 5 MINUTES • SERVES: 4–6

100 g (3½ oz) baby green beans, trimmed

1 red delicious apple, cored, sliced into thin wedges and tossed in lemon juice

¼ celeriac, approximately 400 g (14 oz), peeled and julienned

1 large carrot, peeled and julienned

1 small red onion, halved and thinly sliced into half moons

30 g (1 oz) hazelnuts, toasted, skins removed, roughly chopped

1½ tablespoons finely chopped dill

50 g (1¾ oz) feta cheese, crumbled

Poppyseed dressing

60 ml (2 fl oz/¼ cup) light olive oil

1½ tablespoons caster (superfine) sugar

3 teaspoons lemon juice

1½ tablespoons white wine vinegar

1 teaspoon poppyseeds

To make the dressing, place all the ingredients into a glass jar with a fitted lid. Season with salt and freshly ground black pepper. Shake well and set aside.

Drop the green beans into a saucepan of lightly salted boiling water for 1 minute, then drain and refresh under cold running water to stop the cooking process.

Put the beans, apple, celeriac, carrot, onion, hazelnut and dill in a large bowl. Pour the dressing over and toss to coat. Transfer to a serving platter and scatter the cheese over the top, then serve immediately.

GET AHEAD The poppyseed dressing can be made up to 2 days before serving and refrigerated. The vegetables can be prepared and refrigerated on the morning of serving. Store the apple and celeriac in a bowl of water with the juice of 1 lemon squeezed in to prevent discolouration.

There is much debate over what makes a 'great burger'. I'll throw my two cents in to say that a soft brioche bun and a thin piece of American yellow cheese (the kind from a plastic wrapper) are key. The meat should be minced steak with enough fat to be juicy. I prefer thinner burger patties but if you have any cavemen in your house, you can up the size. The 'secret sauce' here is tomato sauce mixed with chipotle purée, but you can stick to good old ketchup if you're a purist.

DIRTY BURGERS WITH SECRET SAUCE
PREPARATION: 15 MINUTES • COOKING: 10 MINUTES • MAKES: 6

500 g (1 lb 2 oz) minced (ground) beef (try for 20% fat and 80% meat)
1½ tablespoons Worcestershire sauce
2 teaspoons vegetable oil
6 slices yellow American cheese
6 large soft brioche buns, split in half
18 slices Quick Bread & Butter Pickles (see page 34)
6 very thin slices red onion
6 iceberg lettuce leaves

Secret sauce
1 tablespoon chipotle purée
80 ml (2½ fl oz/⅓ cup) tomato sauce (ketchup)
2 tablespoons mayonnaise
2 slices pickles or gherkins, such as Quick Bread & Butter Pickles (see page 34), chopped

Put the meat, Worcestershire sauce and a generous amount of salt and freshly ground black pepper in a bowl and use your hands to combine well. Burgers really need the salt so give it a good teaspoon at least. Shape the meat into 6 thin flat burger patties. Season again and drizzle with the vegetable oil so they don't stick to the grill.

To make the secret sauce, combine all of the ingredients in a bowl and set aside.

Heat a chargrill or barbecue to medium–high. Cook the burger patties over direct heat for 2 minutes each side or until grill marks appear. Top each patty with a slice of cheese and cook for another 30 seconds or until the cheese has melted, then remove from the heat.

Spread a little secret sauce on the base of each bun, then top with the pickles, onion, lettuce and a burger patty. Cover with the bun lid and devour immediately. Serve with Special Salt Fries (see page 32) and extra Quick Bread & Butter Pickles.

GET AHEAD The burger patties can be formed the day before and refrigerated. The secret sauce can made 2 days ahead, covered and refrigerated.

My favourite potato salad dates back to the fifties and I don't think a barbecue is complete without it. Potato salad went out of fashion after being destroyed by grocery stores and bad delis that drowned it in blobs of mayonnaise. The authentic version has to be ice-cold, mixed with tangy sauce and crisp bits of celery and chopped pickle. The perfection lies in tossing the warm potatoes and onions in vinegar first, then letting them cool before mixing in the rest.

GRANNY'S POTATO SALAD WITH PICKLED ONIONS

PREPARATION: 20 MINUTES, PLUS 3 HOURS CHILLING • COOKING: 15 MINUTES • SERVES: 4–6 AS A SIDE DISH

1.5 kg (3 lb 5 oz) waxy red potatoes

1 large red onion, halved and thinly
   sliced into half moons

60 ml (2 fl oz/¼ cup) red wine
   vinegar

200 g (7 oz) mayonnaise

1½ tablespoons dijon mustard

2 celery stalks, finely diced

2 cucumber pickles, finely chopped

2 tablespoons snipped chives

4 hard-boiled eggs, peeled
   and chopped

Put the potatoes in a saucepan of lightly salted cold water over medium heat and bring it to the boil. Simmer for 15 minutes or until tender and a knife can be inserted easily.

Meanwhile, combine the onion and vinegar in a bowl, then cover and set aside.

Drain the potatoes, return them to the pan and allow them to stand for 5 minutes to dry. Using a tea towel (dish towel) to hold the hot potatoes, peel them with a small knife, then cut into bite-size pieces. Add the pieces to the bowl with the onion and vinegar, season to taste with salt and toss to combine. Cover and refrigerate until cold.

Combine the mayonnaise and mustard, then add the mixture to the cold potatoes with the celery, pickles, chives and egg and stir with a spatula until well combined, taking care not to break up the potatoes too much. Season with salt and freshly ground black pepper, then refrigerate the salad for 2 hours or until well chilled.

GET AHEAD The salad will keep for 1 week when covered and refrigerated.

Caesar's anchovy and parmesan spiked dressing is an epiphany on kale leaves. It makes a refreshing change from cos (romaine) lettuce and you can feel chuffed about all those vitamins packed in. The many names for kale can sometimes be confusing: this salad works best using cavolo nero (Americans call it Tuscan kale). It's far more tender than its cousin, curly kale. Ideally, choose the younger pieces sold at farmers' markets or good grocery stores. The recipe also works well with larger leaves, but you need to be sure to discard the tough centre vein. See page 21 for a photograph of this dish, served as a side.

TUSCAN KALE CAESAR SALAD

PREPARATION: 20 MINUTES • COOKING: 10 MINUTES • SERVES: 4–6

3 slices sourdough bread,
   approximately 150 g (5½ oz),
   cut into cubes
2 garlic cloves, thickly sliced
1½ tablespoons olive oil
200 g (7 oz) baby cavolo nero leaves
small handful chopped radicchio
   (optional)
40 g (1½ oz) parmesan cheese, grated

Caesar dressing
1 garlic clove
2 anchovies, rinsed
1 teaspoon salt
3 egg yolks, at room temperature
1½ tablespoons dijon mustard
250 ml (9 fl oz/1 cup) peanut
   (groundnut) or sunflower oil
20 g (¾ oz) parmesan cheese,
   finely grated
3 teaspoons Worcestershire sauce
juice of 3 lemons

Preheat the oven to 210°C (415°F) or 190°C (375°F) fan forced.

Spread the sourdough cubes and sliced garlic on a large baking tray. Drizzle with the oil and season generously with salt and freshly ground black pepper, then toss to combine well. Bake for 8 minutes or until golden and crisp, turning half way through. Remove and discard the garlic, then set the croutons aside.

To make the dressing, put the garlic, anchovy and salt in a mortar and pestle and pound until a paste forms. Scrape the paste into a food processor with the egg yolks and mustard and blend until well combined. With the motor running, gradually add the oil, drop by drop at first, then in a slow steady stream until the mixture is thick and emulsified. Add the parmesan, Worcestershire sauce and three-quarters of the lemon juice and process again. Taste and add the remaining lemon juice if needed. Season to taste with freshly ground black pepper, then set aside.

Coarsely chop the cavolo nero leaves and put them in a large bowl with the radicchio (if using) and the croutons. Pour the caesar dressing over the salad and toss to coat well. Sprinkle the parmesan over the top and serve immediately.

GET AHEAD All of the separate components, including the dressing, can be made the day before serving. Store each component separately in a covered container in the refrigerator. The kale leaves can be prepared and stored in a resealable plastic bag with a paper towel inside. The croutons can be baked and stored in an airtight container.

I love fried chicken but it can be an onerous job waiting for each batch to fry for 20 minutes in the hot oil. If you make it with boneless meat, it only takes about 5–7 minutes for each batch and you still get to enjoy the flaky, spiced buttermilk crust. Dark meat works best and you can leave the skin on or take it off depending on what you like. Use garlic, thyme and lemon zest 'dry brine' the night before to lock in the juices and heighten the flavour and then dip the chicken in the buttermilk and spiced flour. It's delicious cold or hot served as pictured with Tuscan Kale Caesar Salad (see page 19) and ice-cold beer.

BUTTERMILK FRIED BONELESS CHICKEN

PREPARATION: 30 MINUTES, PLUS 12–24 HOURS MARINATING • COOKING: 30 MINUTES • SERVES: 4–6

12 small boneless chicken thighs
   (skin is optional)
300 ml (10½ fl oz) buttermilk
1 egg
1 litre (35 fl oz/4 cups) peanut
   (groundnut) oil, for frying

Dry brine
2 lemons, zest finely grated
1 tablespoon chopped thyme
3 garlic cloves, halved
2 teaspoons sea salt
freshly ground black pepper

Spiced flour
100 g (3½ oz/⅔ cup) plain
   (all-purpose) flour
½ teaspoon garlic salt
½ teaspoon onion salt
1 teaspoon sweet paprika
1 teaspoon chilli powder

To make the dry brine, combine all of the ingredients in a large bowl. Add the chicken, toss to coat well, then cover and refrigerate for 12–24 hours. One hour before cooking, remove the chicken from the refrigerator and allow it to come to room temperature.

To make the spiced flour, combine all the ingredients in a large bowl. Add a good grind of black pepper and mix well.

Put the buttermilk and egg in another bowl and lightly beat with a fork until well combined.

Fill a deep frying pan or heavy-based medium saucepan with the peanut oil and place over medium–high heat until a cube of bread dropped in the oil sizzles in 20 seconds. Line a tray with paper towel and preheat the oven to 200°C (400°F) or 180°C (350°F) fan forced.

While the oil is heating, start to coat the chicken. Dip it in the buttermilk first and then roll it in the spiced flour and place it on a separate tray. Use one hand for dipping in buttermilk and the other for rolling in spiced flour so you don't end up with two hands that look like white gloves. It's a bit messy, so halfway through you might need to wash your hands.

Taking care not to overcrowd the pan, fry 4 pieces of chicken at a time for 5–6 minutes, turning regularly with tongs so they cook evenly on all sides. Bigger pieces may take a minute longer. Drain the chicken on the paper towel, then place it in the oven on a clean tray to keep warm. Continue frying until all the pieces are finished. Serve with wedges of lemon to squeeze over. Instead of the Tuscan Kale Caesar Salad pictured, you could serve the chicken pieces with Celeriac Slaw (see page 14), Garbage Salad (see page 13) or Coleslaw (see page 33).

Originally from South Carolina, pulled pork shoulder is epic. It's slow cooked over a charcoal pit until the meat falls apart, then shredded or 'pulled' and spooned into a soft brioche bun with barbecue sauce, pickles and crisp slaw. Most of us lack a fire pit to slow cook or smoke meat, but it's easily replicated in an oven at a very low temperature.

BARBECUE PULLED PORK SANDWICHES

PREPARATION: 10 MINUTES • COOKING: 5 HOURS • SERVES: 6–8

2.5 kg (5 lb 8 oz) boneless pork
   shoulder with most of the top
   fat removed
2 tablespoons olive oil
12–16 brioche buns or soft rolls

Quick Bread & Butter Pickles
   (see page 34), Home-made Smoky
   Molasses Barbecue Sauce (see
   page 33) and Sweet & Sour Coleslaw
   (see page 33), to serve

Spice rub
2 teaspoons Spanish paprika
   (pimenton)
2 teaspoons mustard powder
1 teaspoon garlic salt
1 teaspoon onion salt

Preheat the oven to 150°C (300°F) or 130°C (250°F) fan forced. To make the spice rub, combine all the ingredients in a small bowl.

Rub the pork with the olive oil. Heat a heavy-based non-stick frying pan over high heat until very hot. Sear the meat until golden on all sides, then place on a wire rack in a roasting pan. Allow to cool slightly and then apply the spice rub all over the meat and season with freshly ground black pepper. Pour 250 ml (9 fl oz/1 cup) of water into the pan, cover very tightly with foil and cook for 5 hours or until the meat is almost falling apart.

Remove the meat from the pan, then pour the juices into a glass jug and set aside.

Using two forks, shred the pork and return it to the roasting pan. Discard the fat from the juices (it will float to the top) and pour 125 ml (4 fl oz/½ cup) of the juices over the pork and mix well. Keep warm.

Divide the warm shredded pork among the brioche buns. Top with bread and butter pickles and a spoonful of barbecue sauce, then add a good spoonful of coleslaw and sandwich together. Serve with either Granny's Potato Salad (see page 18), Garbage Salad (see page 13), or Tuscan Kale Caesar Salad (see page 19).

GET AHEAD The meat can be roasted, shredded and mixed with the juices up to 2 days ahead. Reheat in a 200°C (400°F) oven, covered in foil, for 20 minutes. You can also reheat with the barbecue sauce mixed in. The barbecue sauce can be made 2 weeks ahead, covered and refrigerated.

Coffee isn't the first ingredient to pop into your mind when making a rub for steak but it is magic when combined with spices and sugar. Use your favourite cut of beef and serve with the sauce and fries or pop the meat and sauce into a bun with a handful of rocket (arugula). If you're not up to making home-made mayo, add the lemon and Worcestershire sauce to 200 g (7 oz) of mayonnaise for a quick cheat.

COFFEE-RUBBED SKIRT STEAK WITH WORCESTERSHIRE STEAK SAUCE

PREPARATION: 20 MINUTES, PLUS 10 MINUTES RESTING • COOKING: 5 MINUTES • SERVES: 4–6

900 g (2 lb) beef skirt (onglet), flank or bavette, cut into 4–6 steaks
3 teaspoons olive oil
3 teaspoons finely ground coffee beans
3 teaspoons chilli powder, such as Aleppo pepper
3 teaspoons smoked paprika
3 teaspoons soft brown sugar
1 teaspoon mustard powder
1 teaspoon salt

Worcestershire steak sauce
1 egg yolk, at room temperature
1 teaspoon dijon mustard
½ garlic clove, crushed
100 ml (3½ fl oz) sunflower oil
juice of ½ lemon
1 tablespoon Worcestershire sauce
1 teaspoon snipped chives

To make the steak sauce, place the egg yolk, mustard and garlic in a small food processor and combine well. (If you don't have a small food processor, then either double the recipe and use the remainder for sandwiches, or use a handheld whisk instead.) With the motor running, gradually add the oil, drop by drop at first and then in a slow steady stream until the mixture is thick and emulsified. Stir in the lemon juice, Worcestershire sauce, chives and plenty of freshly ground black pepper. Transfer to a bowl, cover and refrigerate until serving.

Preheat a chargrill or barbecue to high. Rub the steaks with the oil. Combine the coffee, chilli, paprika, sugar, mustard powder and salt in a small bowl, then sprinkle on both sides of the steaks. Grind a little black pepper over each steak, then cook for 2–3 minutes on each side or until done to your liking. If the steaks are thicker than about 4 cm (1½ inches), cook for another minute on each side. Transfer to a platter, cover loosely with foil and rest for 10 minutes before slicing.

Serve the meat with the Worcestershire steak sauce and Special Salt Fries (see page 32) or other fries.

GET AHEAD The Worcestershire steak sauce can be made the day before and stored in the refrigerator in an airtight container. The garlic can be strong, so perhaps leave it out until just before serving. The rub can be put together a couple of days before and stored in a screw-top jar. You can marinate the meat with the rub on in the refrigerator overnight. Allow the meat to come to room temperature before cooking.

Every couple of years we stay in the Outer Banks of North Carolina, USA, with my sister's family. The only thing that trumps the wild southern beaches is the gargantuan fresh prawns. Shrimp boils are the local specialty: shrimp poached in beer and aromatic spices. Spread out lots of newspapers, then peel, dip and eat.

SPICED SHRIMP BOIL WITH HORSERADISH COCKTAIL SAUCE

PREPARATION: 10 MINUTES • COOKING: 5 MINUTES • SERVES: 4–6 AS A STARTER OR SNACK

80 g (2¾ oz) Old Bay® Seasoning (see below), plus extra for sprinkling
750 ml (26 fl oz/3 cups) beer
10 black peppercorns
4 bay leaves
1 onion, quartered
1 kg (2 lb 4 oz) raw large prawns (shrimp), unpeeled

Cocktail sauce
250 ml (9 fl oz/1 cup) tomato sauce (ketchup)
1½ tablespoons grated horseradish
juice of 1 lemon
1 teaspoon hot chilli sauce
1 teaspoon Worcestershire sauce
1 teaspoon celery salt

OLD BAY SEASONING

A classic American spice mix that's been around since the fifties, its primary flavour is celery salt. Just like Worcestershire sauce, it 'tastes good in everything'. If you can't buy it, then whip up a batch of your own. Combine 1½ tablespoons celery salt, ½ teaspoon paprika and ¼ teaspoon each of cayenne pepper, mustard powder, ground mace, ground cinnamon, ground cardamom, ground allspice, ground cloves and ground ginger. Put the mixture in a small jar, seal and store in a cool dark place for up to 6 months.

To make the cocktail sauce, combine all of the ingredients in a small bowl and refrigerate, covered, until serving.

Put 2 litres (70 fl oz/8 cups) water in a large saucepan over high heat and add the Old Bay Seasoning, beer, peppercorns, bay leaves and onion. Bring to the boil. Add the prawns and cook for 3 minutes or just until they turn pink. Drain and sprinkle with the extra Old Bay Seasoning.

Serve the prawns while still warm on a big platter with newspapers spread out on the table to catch the shells. Dip the peeled prawns into the cocktail sauce.

GET AHEAD The cocktail sauce can be made 3 days before, covered and then refrigerated.

Nothing beats a grilled sausage at a summer barbecue. A home-made relish can make all the difference. My favourite is home-made pickled baby peppers: this relish can be used to adorn sausages, hot dogs or submarine sandwiches. If you have access to a good brand of relish, then by all means buy it, but if not, whip up a batch of your own.

GRILLED SAUSAGES WITH CARAMELISED ONION & PICKLED BABY PEPPERS

PREPARATION: 20 MINUTES, PLUS OVERNIGHT MARINATING • COOKING: 10 MINUTES • SERVES: 4–6

1 tablespoon olive oil
1 onion, sliced
4–6 hot Italian pork and fennel
  sausages or bratwurst

6 soft buns, split down the middle
yellow American mustard and tomato
  sauce (ketchup), to serve

Pickled baby peppers
250 g (9 oz) mini capsicums
  (peppers), seeded and sliced
  1 cm (⅜ inch) thick
2 small French shallots, sliced
100 g (3½ oz) caster (superfine)
  sugar
250 ml (9 fl oz/1 cup) white wine
  vinegar
3 teaspoons yellow mustard seeds
1 teaspoon sea salt
2 teaspoons chilli flakes, crushed

To make the pickled peppers, combine the peppers and shallot in a bowl. Put the remaining ingredients in a saucepan with 200 ml (7 fl oz) of water. Bring to the boil, then pour over the peppers. Stand until cooled to room temperature, then cover and refrigerate for at least 3 hours and up to 2 weeks.

Heat the olive oil in a small saucepan over low to medium heat. Add the onion and season to taste, then cook, stirring frequently, for 10 minutes or until golden and caramelised. Remove from the heat and set aside.

Heat a barbecue or chargrill over direct heat. Cook the sausages for 5–6 minutes or until cooked through. Serve the sausages in the split buns with separate bowls of the caramelised onion, yellow American mustard, tomato sauce and the pickled peppers to spoon over. Have plenty of napkins on hand.

GET AHEAD Make the pickled peppers up to 2 weeks ahead and keep covered and refrigerated. On the morning of serving, caramelise the onions then cover and refrigerate. Reheat the onions in a frying pan before serving with the grilled sausages.

These ribs will make you happy for two reasons: (1) they are slow cooked to perfection and (2) the lip-smacking sauce—made from Mexican chillies, tomatoes and tamarind—is seriously tasty. If you're short on time, use barbecue sauce. Be sure to get baby back ribs, as they have much more meat than spare ribs.

FALL-APART BABY BACK RIBS WITH MAPLE CHIPOTLE SAUCE

PREPARATION: 10 MINUTES • COOKING: 2 HOURS 10 MINUTES • SERVES: 4–6

45 g (1½ oz/¼ cup) soft brown sugar

1½ tablespoons smoked paprika

1½ tablespoons mustard powder

1½ tablespoons mild chilli powder

4 racks pork baby back ribs

Maple chipotle sauce

3 roma (plum) tomatoes, halved lengthways

1 large onion, thickly sliced

8 garlic cloves, unpeeled

2 tablespoons chipotle purée

100 g (3½ oz) tamarind purée

2 tablespoons soft brown sugar

60 ml (2 fl oz/¼ cup) maple syrup

1½ tablespoons cider vinegar

1 teaspoon salt

Preheat the oven to 170°C (325°F) or 150°C (300°F) fan forced.

Combine the sugar and spices in a bowl, then rub all over the ribs. Put the ribs on a wire rack in a large roasting pan. Pour 150 ml (5 fl oz) of water into the bottom of the pan, cover tightly with foil and roast for 2 hours or until the ribs are nearly falling apart. Drain and discard the cooking liquid.

Meanwhile, to make the sauce, place the tomato and onion on a baking tray, under a preheated oven grill (broiler) and cook for 6–8 minutes until charred all over. Put the garlic in a dry frying pan and cook over medium heat until the skins are blackened. Peel the garlic and put it in a food processor with the tomato and onion and all of the remaining ingredients. Add 2 tablespoons of water and process until smooth. Transfer to a clean bowl.

To serve, preheat a barbecue or oven to 220°C (425°F) or 200°C (400°F) fan forced. Cook the ribs, basting regularly with the sauce for 3–4 minutes on both sides or until golden and sticky. Serve with Coleslaw with creamy lime, chilli & coriander dressing (see page 33), Grilled Corn (see page 67) and Granny's Potato Salad (see page 18).

GET AHEAD The ribs can be slow roasted up to 2 days ahead, covered and refrigerated. The sauce can be made up to 1 week ahead, covered and refrigerated.

SLOW OR FAST COOKING You can slow cook these ribs in the oven but also think about a pressure cooker. Fold the ribs up inside the pot after rubbing with the spices, but don't fill more than half of the pot. It's best to do two batches. Add the water and then cook for 30 minutes on high. You will have melting tender meat in no time. Use the short (4-hour) time on the slow cooker if you want to leave them and go. Use half the amount of water in the base.

When I was growing up in Wisconsin, the sweet summer peaches were amazing and my sisters and I would make pies and shortcakes with them. I now live in the UK where the peaches aren't so flavourful, so I cheat and use tinned ones. They're tinned when they're ripe, so that you get perfect sweetness and you don't have to peel or stone the fruit: definitely nothing to sniff at. Feel free to use other fruit, such as plums, nectarines and blueberries.

PEACH & RASPBERRY MINI PIES

PREPARATION: 30 MINUTE, PLUS 1 HOUR CHILLING • COOKING: 40 MINUTES • MAKES: 12

500 g (1 lb 2 oz) shortcrust pastry
9 small peaches, peeled, stoned and diced (or use two 400 g tins, drained well)
150 g (5½ oz/1¼ cups) fresh raspberries
100 g (3½ oz) caster (superfine) sugar
18 g (⅝ oz) cornflour (cornstarch)
1 teaspoon vanilla bean paste
finely grated zest of 1 lemon
1 large egg yolk, lightly beaten
raw (demerara) sugar, for sprinkling

Preheat the oven to 210°C (415°F) or 190°C (375°F) fan forced. Roll out 375 g (13 oz) of the pastry on a lightly floured work surface until it is about 3 mm (⅛ inch) thick. Using a 10 cm (4 inch) pastry cutter, cut out 12 circles and press them into a regular-size muffin tin. Roll out the remaining pastry and cut out twelve 7 cm (2¾ inch) circles. Cut out little stars from the dough to make vents. If you don't have a star cutter just use a knife or cut small circles. Chill the pastry lids in the refrigerator while you make the filling.

Combine the peaches, raspberries, caster sugar, cornflour, vanilla bean paste and lemon zest in a large bowl and divide evenly between the pies. Brush the edges of the lids with egg yolk and place one on top of each pie, using your fingers to press the edges together. Put the muffin tray in the freezer for 1 hour before baking. This will firm up the dough so that it cooks without leaking.

Just before baking, brush the tops with the remaining egg yolk and sprinkle with the raw sugar. Bake in the lower third of the oven for 30–40 minutes or until the pastry is golden. Remove from the oven. If some of the juice leaks out, just wipe it off with paper towel. After the pies have cooled for 5 minutes, run a small knife around the edges to keep the juice from sticking. Allow to cool in the tins for another 10 minutes then remove.

GET AHEAD Prepare the tarts in full on the morning of serving. Alternatively, you can freeze the raw pies and bake from frozen, adding an extra 5 minutes cooking time.

EXTRAS & SIMPLE SIDES

SPECIAL SALT FRIES

PREPARATION: 10 MINUTES • COOKING: 25 MINUTES • SERVES: 4–6

Preheating the oven to a very high temperature ensures that these baked 'fries' come out crisp. The special salt and lemon zest gives them an extra kick of flavour.

5 large red-skinned potatoes, unpeeled
2 tablespoons light olive oil
¼ teaspoon each of garlic salt, onion salt, ground coriander, ground smoked paprika
finely grated zest of 1 lemon

Preheat the oven to 240°C (475°F) or 220°C (425°F) fan forced.

Cut the potatoes into chips, about 2 cm (¾ inch) thick. Rinse the starch off in a large bowl of water, then pat dry well with a tea towel (dish towel).

Spread the potatoes in a single layer on one large baking tray, or two smaller ones. You need to give the chips space otherwise they steam instead of crisping up. Drizzle with the olive oil, then scatter with the combined spices and toss to coat well. Bake for 20 minutes, tossing halfway through the cooking time, then sprinkle with the lemon zest and bake for another 5 minutes or until golden and crisp.

Variation: For cheese fries, add a handful of shredded parmesan to the fries in the last 5 minutes of cooking to melt over the top.

GET AHEAD The potatoes can be cut on the morning of serving, and stored in iced water to keep them crisp and prevent discolouring. Dry well and carry on with the recipe just before serving.

HOME-MADE SMOKY MOLASSES BARBECUE SAUCE

PREPARATION: 10 MINUTES • COOKING: 20 MINUTES • MAKES: 900 ML (31 FL OZ)

Making your own barbecue sauce is infinitely better than buying commercial products. It doesn't take long and you might just gain a following.

2 tablespoons olive oil
1 small onion, finely chopped
3 garlic cloves, chopped
150 ml (5 fl oz) apple cider vinegar
125 g (4½ oz/⅔ cup, lightly packed)
  dark brown sugar
2 teaspoons mustard powder
2 teaspoons smoked paprika
2 teaspoons celery salt
3 teaspoons hot chilli powder
2½ tablespoons Worcestershire sauce
3 teaspoons chipotle purée
2½ tablespoons tomato paste (concentrated purée)
500 ml (17 fl oz/2 cups) tomato passata
  (puréed tomatoes)
1½ tablespoons molasses or dark treacle syrup

Heat the oil in a large saucepan over medium heat. Add the onion and garlic and stir constantly for 5 minutes or until soft. Add all the remaining ingredients, bring to the boil, then reduce the heat to low and simmer for 15 minutes or until the sauce coats the back of a spoon. Remove from the heat, pour immediately into sterilised jars and seal. Allow to cool, then store in the refrigerator for up to 2 weeks.

COLESLAW TWO WAYS

PREPARATION: 10 MINUTES, PLUS 1 HOUR SOAKING • SERVES: 4–6 AS A SIDE

Coleslaw has re-emerged after being assassinated by generations of bad cooks. Here are two of my best dressings, one oldie and a new version with chilli and lime. Crisp the vegetables in iced water before dressing: it makes all the difference.

¼ head each red and white cabbage, thinly sliced
2 carrots, peeled and julienned
1 small red onion, finely chopped
1 celery heart, thinly sliced
8 small red radishes, thinly sliced or quartered
1 red capsicum (pepper), halved, seeds and
  membrane discarded, cut into thin slices

Creamy lime, chilli and coriander dressing
150 g (5½ oz) mayonnaise
juice and finely grated zest of 1 lime
3 teaspoons apple cider vinegar
1 small mild green chilli, seeded, thinly sliced
2 tablespoons finely chopped coriander (cilantro)

Sweet and sour dressing
2 tablespoons white wine vinegar
2 tablespoons soft brown sugar
1 teaspoon mustard powder
¼ teaspoon each mustard seeds, celery seeds
  and poppyseeds
60 ml (2 fl oz/¼ cup) vegetable oil

Put all of the vegetables in a large bowl of iced water for 1 hour to crisp up. Drain well and pat dry with a clean tea towel (dish towel), then transfer to a large serving bowl.

To make the dressing, put all of the dressing ingredients in a bowl with a large pinch of salt and whisk until well combined and the sugar has dissolved. Pour the dressing over the vegetables, toss well and refrigerate until serving.

GET AHEAD The dressed coleslaw will keep for 2 days, covered and refrigerated.

ICEBERG WEDGES WITH BUTTERMILK RANCH DRESSING

PREPARATION: 10 MINUTES • COOKING: 10 MINUTES • SERVES: 4–6 AS A SIDE

Among lettuces, iceberg doesn't rank the highest in nutrients but no other salad greens can come close to its dense juicy bite. Ranch dressing might be a flashback to the seventies, when dressings were made with powdered mixes, but it's just come back into fashion. The real deal is delicious and uses buttermilk so it's low in fat. Whisk up a batch and bring any lettuces or tomatoes to life.

6 rashers rindless bacon
1 iceberg lettuce
100 g (3½ oz) cherry tomatoes, halved
1 small red onion, sliced into rings

Buttermilk ranch dressing
80 ml (2½ fl oz/⅓ cup) buttermilk
2 tablespoons mayonnaise
1 tablespoon white wine vinegar
½ garlic clove, crushed
1 tablespoon snipped chives
1 teaspoon salt

Set a dry frying pan over medium heat, add the bacon and cook until very crisp. Drain on paper towel, then crumble into tiny pieces. Set aside.

To make the buttermilk ranch dressing, put all of the ingredients and a good grind of black pepper in a bowl and whisk well. Cut the lettuce in half and then into smaller wedges, about 8 in total. Place the wedges on a platter with the tomatoes. Just before serving, pour the dressing over, sprinkle with the crumbled bacon and top with the onion rings.

GET AHEAD The dressing will keep for 2 days, covered and refrigerated.

QUICK BREAD & BUTTER PICKLES

PREPARATION: 15 MINUTES, PLUS 3 HOURS MARINATING • COOKING: 5 MINUTES • MAKES: 500 ML (17 FL OZ/2 CUPS)

These classic pickles are as American as peanut butter and one of the products I sorely miss now that I am living in London. It's forced me to make my own and they aren't far off the jars of yellow-hued slices sold all over America. Baby kirby cucumbers or gherkins work best for this but I have also used the small Persian or Lebanese cucumbers.

400 g (14 oz) Lebanese (short) or kirby cucumbers, cut into 1 cm (⅜ inch) thick slices
1 onion, cut into 1 cm (⅜ inch) thick slices
2 tablespoons rock salt or flaked sea salt
300 ml (10½ fl oz) apple cider vinegar
250 ml (9 fl oz/1 cup) water
150 g (5½ oz/⅔ cup) caster (superfine) sugar
pinch of ground turmeric
pinch of celery seeds
pinch of dried red chilli flakes, crushed
1½ tablespoons yellow or brown mustard seeds

Put the cucumbers, onion slices and salt in a bowl, cover with iced water and soak for 1 hour. Drain well.

Meanwhile, combine the vinegar, water, sugar, turmeric, celery seeds, chilli flakes and mustard seeds in a small saucepan over medium heat. Bring to the boil, then simmer for 5 minutes. Remove from the heat and stand until cooled to room temperature.

Transfer the cucumber and onion mixture to a 500 ml (17 fl oz/2 cup) jar or sealable plastic container, pour the syrup over, cover and seal. Refrigerate for at least 3 hours before using. Pickles will keep, refrigerated, for 2 weeks.

MEXICO &
SOUTH AMERICA

FIERY TACOS
& ICY CEVICHE

If I had to choose my top dishes, one of them would be Peruvian ceviche. Its acidic tang is clean and utterly fresh. I love the way you can change the flavours using tropical fruit, tomatoes, soy sauce or chillies. The fish you choose is vital. It can't be too oily, soft or bony. Halibut, barramundi cod, redfish or tuna are my favourites: almost no waste, mild flavour and easy to slice.

There are many opinions about how long you 'cook' the fish (it's still raw but the proteins change colour). While some recipes marinate for hours, others are served in a flash with the 'leche de tigre' (the cloudy liquid that appears when the fish is covered in the citrus juices). With white fish I marinate it for at least one hour, then drain and re-dress so it's not fishy. The flesh turns a beautiful iridescent white, but with tuna it's best to marinate for just a few minutes to maintain the crimson colour.

TRES CEVICHES

400 g (14 oz) skinless, boneless
   halibut or barramundi cod
juice of 1 orange
200 ml (7 fl oz) lime juice
1 teaspoon caster (superfine) sugar
1 teaspoon salt
1 small red onion, very thinly sliced
½ baby pineapple, peeled, cored,
   cut into 1 cm (⅜ inch) pieces
1 thumb-size green chilli, halved,
   seeded, finely chopped
1 handful of coriander (cilantro)
   leaves, to scatter

Baked Tortilla Chips (see page 66)
   and lime wedges, to serve

Chilli drizzle
1 teaspoon chipotle purée
3 teaspoons apple cider vinegar
3 teaspoons soft brown sugar

1 HALIBUT CEVICHE WITH PINEAPPLE & CHILLI DRIZZLE
PREPARATION: 20 MINUTES, PLUS 1 HOUR MARINATING • SERVES: 4

The tangy chipotle chilli sauce takes this ceviche to another level. Make a big platter to eat with crisp baked corn tortillas and your friends will love you.

Using a large sharp knife, cut the fish against the grain into paper-thin slices. Put the slices in a shallow non-metallic container and pour in the orange juice and 140 ml (4⅝ fl oz) of the lime juice. Add the sugar and salt. Gently combine, then cover and refrigerate for 1 hour.

Meanwhile, put the onion in a small bowl with 125 ml (4 fl oz/½ cup) of lightly salted iced water. Stand for 10 minutes, then drain.

To make the chilli drizzle, combine all of the ingredients in a small bowl with a pinch of salt.

Drain the fish well, dress with salt and the remaining lime juice, then arrange the fish and pineapple pieces on four plates or one serving platter. Scatter with the drained onions, chopped chilli and coriander leaves. Drizzle the chilli sauce around the edge of the plates and serve with Baked Tortilla Chips and lime wedges.

CONTINUED

TRES CEVICHES (CONTINUED)

400 g (14 oz) halibut, scallops,
  or other firm mild white fish,
  cut into 2 cm (¾ inch) pieces
200 ml (7 fl oz) lime juice
juice of 1 orange
1 teaspoon caster (superfine) sugar
1 teaspoon salt
50 ml (1¾ fl oz) coconut cream
1 tablespoon yuzu or grapefruit juice
1 firm, ripe mango, cut into 2 cm
  (¾ inch) pieces
1½ tablespoons finely chopped
  red onion
1 thumb-size red chilli, thinly sliced
small handful of coriander (cilantro)
  sprigs, chopped
1 large navel orange, peeled and
  segmented

Baked Tortilla Chips (see page 66),
  to serve

YUZU

Similar in shape and size to tangerines, yuzu are Japanese citrus fruits coveted for their floral scented zest and juice. The unique taste lifts dressings, dipping sauces and marinades with an assertive freshness. The flavour is similar to a medley of grapefruit, lime and orange juices, so if you can't find yuzu you can mix these in equal parts as a substitute. Pure juice is sold in bottles in Asian grocery stores and large supermarkets.

 ## TROPICAL CEVICHE WITH COCONUT CREAM & RED CHILLI
PREPARATION: 20 MINUTES, PLUS 1 HOUR MARINATING • SERVES: 4

You can use any white fish with this combination but feel free to swap in scallops, redfish or barramundi cod. The sharp taste of yuzu (or grapefruit) cuts the creamy coconut to make a captivating dressing.

Place the fish in a bowl with the lime juice and orange juice, sugar and salt. Combine well, then cover and refrigerate for 1 hour. Drain the fish, then toss in a bowl with the coconut cream and yuzu or grapefruit juice. Add the remaining ingredients and toss to combine well. Serve in small glasses with Baked Tortilla Chips.

GET AHEAD Slice the fish earlier in the day and store in the refrigerator between layers of baking paper, loosely covered with plastic wrap. (Plastic wrap makes fish sweat, so don't cover too tightly.) Squeeze the oranges and limes, make the dressing and chop any vegetables or herbs. Keep everything separate and then marinate and mix shortly before serving.

juice of 1 orange

170 ml (5½ fl oz/⅔ cup) lime juice

2 teaspoons caster (superfine) sugar

2 teaspoons salt

400 g (14 oz) sashimi-grade skinless
tuna fillet

2 tablespoons coarsely chopped
coriander (cilantro) leaves

Baked Tortilla Chips (see page 66),
to serve

Salsa criolla

1 red onion, sliced into thin
half moons

1 thumb-size green chilli, sliced into
thin rings

1 red banana chilli or romero pepper,
halved, seeded, thinly sliced

1½ tablespoons lime juice

1½ tablespoons white wine vinegar

TUNA CEVICHE WITH SALSA CRIOLLA

PREPARATION: 20 MINUTES, PLUS 40 MINUTES MARINATING • SERVES: 4

Buy tuna fillet that is the middle of the loin, free from the sinewy fat marbling as this is too chewy for ceviche or sashimi. Salsa criolla is a Peruvian salad in which the onions are soaked in salted iced water to remove the harsh taste and then tossed with fresh lime, chillies and coriander. It's shockingly good with the raw tuna, scooped up with the crisp tortilla chips: this version is shown in the photograph on page 43. Be sure to make some chilly caipirinhas to go alongside and quench everyone's thirst.

To make the salsa criolla, put the onion in a small bowl, cover with 125 ml (4 fl oz/½ cup) of lightly salted iced water and stand for 10 minutes. Drain and pat dry with paper towel, then combine with the remaining salsa ingredients and stand at room temperature for 10 minutes before serving.

Just before serving, mix together the lime juice, orange juice, caster sugar and salt. Cut the tuna into small slices, about 5 mm (¼ inch) thick, and toss in the mixture with the coriander. Arrange the slices on a serving platter or on individual plates. Top each with the salsa criolla and extra coriander leaves if you like. Serve with Baked Tortilla Chips.

Opposite: Baked Tortilla Chips (page 66).
This page: Tuna Ceviche with Salsa Criolla (page 41).

Palm hearts, with their strange tubular shape, don't overwhelm you at first glance but don't underestimate their genius taste. It's sort of a cross between an artichoke and celery. Pair them with avocados and tomatoes for quick salsas and salads. The young shoots are farmed and harvested before they grow into palm trees so it is completely ethical to buy and eat them.

HEART OF PALM SALAD WITH LIME & HONEY DRESSING

PREPARATION: 15 MINUTES • COOKING: 5 MINUTES • SERVES: 4

125 g (4½ oz) green beans, trimmed, cut into 2.5 cm (1 inch) lengths
1 small red onion, halved and thinly sliced into half moons
2 avocados, chopped
½ lemon
400 g (14 oz) tin of palm hearts, drained, sliced into 3 cm (1¼ inch) pieces
2 navel oranges, peeled, segmented
1 tablespoon pepitas (pumpkin seeds), lightly toasted, salted

Dressing
50 ml (1¾ fl oz) extra virgin olive oil
juice of 2 limes
3 teaspoons white wine vinegar
3 teaspoons honey
1 tablespoon chopped coriander (cilantro) leaves

Cook the green beans in a saucepan of lightly salted boiling water for 1–2 minutes or until tender but still firm to the bite. Drain and refresh under cold running water. Drain again, pat dry on a clean tea towel (dish towel) and put the beans in a large salad bowl.

Put the onion and avocado in separate bowls, squeeze the lemon juice over the top of both and stand for 5 minutes. Drain, then add to the salad bowl. Add the palm hearts and orange segments and toss gently to combine.

To make the dressing, combine all the ingredients in a small jar with a fitted lid. Season with salt and freshly ground black pepper, then shake well to combine. Just before serving, pour the dressing over the salad and scatter over the pepitas.

GET AHEAD Blanch the beans, chop the vegetables and make the dressing earlier in the day. Keep them separate, cover and refrigerate. Drizzle some citrus juice over the avocado to keep it from discolouring. Toss everything together just before serving.

Their origins were in Spain, but empanadas are eaten all over South America. Each country has its best-loved variations made with beef, seafood, chicken or cheese. This piquant chicken version with chillies and raisins is from Argentina and is baked instead of the usual deep-frying.

SPICED CHICKEN EMPANADAS
PREPARATION: 30 MINUTES, PLUS 1 HOUR CHILLING • COOKING: 45 MINUTES • MAKES: 12

1 tablespoon olive oil

350 g (12 oz) boneless, skinless chicken thighs

2 onions, finely chopped

3 garlic cloves, finely chopped

1 teaspoon chilli flakes

1 teaspoon ground cumin

1 teaspoon ground fennel

3 teaspoons smoked paprika

3 teaspoons baby capers in brine, drained

1 tablespoon tomato paste (concentrated purée)

1½ tablespoons raisins

Pastry

350 g (12 oz/2⅓ cups) plain (all-purpose) flour

175 g (6 oz) unsalted butter, cold, chopped

1 teaspoon salt

1 egg, lightly beaten

3 teaspoons white wine vinegar

GET AHEAD Make the empanadas and put them on a tray between two pieces of baking paper, cover with plastic wrap and refrigerate for up to 2 days. Bake just before serving. These also freeze well, so wrap them as for refrigerating and allow them to thaw in the refrigerator on the day of serving.

To make the filling, heat 2 teaspoons of oil in a large frying pan over high heat. Season the chicken, then cook on both sides until browned. Remove from the pan and drain off any excess fat. Reserve the pan and cut the chicken into 2 cm (¾ inch) pieces. Add the remaining oil, onion and garlic to the reserved pan and cook over medium heat for 5–6 minutes or until the onion is soft. Add all of the remaining ingredients, including the chicken, and 2 tablespoons of water. Season with salt and pepper and simmer for 5 minutes so the flavours meld together. Remove from the heat, spread onto a tray and stand until completely cooled. It's a good idea to put the tray in the freezer to cool it down quickly.

Meanwhile, to make the pastry, put the flour, butter and salt into a food processor and pulse until the mixture resembles fine breadcrumbs. Add the egg and vinegar and process until the pastry just comes together. Turn the dough out onto a work surface, shape into a ball, then wrap in plastic wrap and refrigerate for 30 minutes.

Line two baking trays with baking paper and set aside. Roll out the dough on a lightly floured work surface about 4 mm (³⁄₁₆ inch) thick. Using a 10 cm (4 inch) diameter pastry cutter, stamp out 12 rounds from the pastry. Place on the prepared trays and refrigerate for 30 minutes.

Preheat the oven to 200°C (400°F) or 180°C (350°F) fan forced. Put a heavy-based baking tray in the oven to preheat.

Place a portion of the cooled filling on one half of each circle and fold the pastry over the filling. Pinch the edges together to seal well, then use a fork to press them together or fold the pressed edges over like petals.

Lay the empanadas on a large piece of baking paper and then on the preheated baking tray. Bake for 20–25 minutes or until golden and crisp. Serve warm with any of the three sauces in the Brazilian Churrasco recipe (see page 52).

Brazilians call these 'malagueta prawns', from the local name for the small 'piri piri' chillies in the sauce. I love the sauce brushed on butterflied chicken, beef ribs or pork chops on the grill. At first glance you may think it will be hot, but roasting the chillies first and mixing with vinegar tames them for a beautiful mouth-puckery sauce. Splitting the shell down the back of the prawn makes it easier to eat after grilling and keeps the flesh from drying out. Serve as a starter or with rice for a main meal.

PEEL-&-EAT PIRI PIRI PRAWNS
PREPARATION: 15 MINUTES • COOKING: 10 MINUTES • SERVES: 4–6 AS A STARTER

20 large raw prawns (shrimp),
   unpeeled
lemon wedges, to serve

Piri piri sauce
4 finger-length fresh red chillies
8 garlic cloves, unpeeled
2 teaspoons tomato paste
   (concentrated purée)
juice of 2 lemons
45 ml (1½ fl oz) red wine vinegar
2 teaspoons smoked paprika
1½ tablespoons olive oil

To make the piri piri sauce, place the chillies and garlic in a small frying pan over medium heat and dry-fry for 5 minutes or until blackened. When cool enough to handle, peel the garlic and chillies and remove the chilli seeds. Put them in a blender with the remaining ingredients and season with salt. Purée until the sauce is smooth.

Preheat a barbecue or a chargrill pan to medium–high. If using wooden skewers, soak them in water for at least 10 minutes to prevent them from burning during cooking.

Remove the heads and legs from the prawns. Using kitchen scissors, cut a slit along the back of each prawn about 5 cm (2 inches) long and carefully remove the digestive tract. Put the prawns in a bowl, add half the piri piri sauce and toss to coat well. Thread one prawn onto each skewer, then cook for about 3 minutes on each side until grill marks appear and the shells turn a deep pink. Serve with the remaining piri piri sauce and lemon wedges to squeeze over.

GET AHEAD Make the piri piri sauce up to 2 days ahead, and refrigerate in a covered container. Split the backs of the prawns earlier in the day and store them in a bowl lined with paper towel. Marinate and grill just before serving.

All South American countries have their particular method of 'churrasco', which is the Spanish word for grill. In Brazil the cuts of meat are skewered and slowly roasted on a rotisserie over charcoal. As the sides cook, the meat is thinly sliced off, like a kebab. Since most of us have pretty basic barbecues, I've devised a marinade that pimps up any cut of meat no matter what grill you use. Try it with one or all three of the sauces.

BRAZILIAN CHURRASCO WITH THREE SAUCES
PREPARATION: 15 MINUTES, PLUS OVERNIGHT MARINATING • COOKING: 10 MINUTES • SERVES: 4–6

1 kg (2 lb 4 oz) beef skirt (onglet),
   flank or bavette steak
3 garlic cloves, crushed
juice of 2 limes
1½ tablespoons red wine vinegar
1½ tablespoons Worcestershire sauce
1 small onion, grated
2 teaspoons cumin seeds
3 teaspoons Aleppo pepper
   or chilli flakes
1½ tablespoons olive oil, plus extra
   for drizzling

ALEPPO PEPPER

Also known as pul biber, this ground spice is made of dried Turkish chillies that pack a fruity, smoky taste but aren't too spicy. The seeds are removed before grinding, so the pepper won't overpower your cooking with too much heat. Once you've tried it, it will become your go-to chilli powder. Substitute crushed red chilli flakes if you don't have any Aleppo pepper.

Cut the steak into 4–6 even portions and season well with salt and freshly ground black pepper on both sides, then put the steak in a shallow non-metallic dish. Put the remaining ingredients in a small bowl and mix well. Pour the marinade over the steaks, turn to coat, then cover and refrigerate overnight. Remove from the refrigerator 1 hour before cooking to bring the meat back to room temperature.

Preheat a barbecue or chargrill pan until very hot. Remove the meat from the marinade and pat dry on paper towel, then drizzle with a little extra oil and season with extra salt and pepper. Thread two long metal skewers through two of the steaks and repeat with the others. Grill for 3–4 minutes on each side or until cooked to your liking. Rest in a warm place for 10 minutes, then slice and serve with the sauces (recipes on the following page).

GET AHEAD Marinate the meat up to 24 hours ahead. The sauces are best made earlier in the day, covered and refrigerated; however, the herbs in the Chimichurri Sauce (see page 52) will stay brighter if it is made 1–2 hours before serving.

CONTINUED

¾ cup coriander (cilantro), leaves
 and stems
1 thumb-size green chilli, stem
 and seeds removed
2 spring onions (scallions), chopped
1 garlic clove, finely chopped
juice of 1 lime
2 tablespoons mayonnaise
2 tablespoons sour cream

1 CREAMY AJI VERDE SAUCE
PREPARATION: 10 MINUTES • MAKES: 250 ML (9 FL OZ/1 CUP)

This creamy sauce gets its triple tang from the lime.

Process all of the ingredients in a blender until smooth, then pour into a serving bowl and season with salt and freshly ground black pepper.

1 cup coriander (cilantro) leaves
1 cup flat-leaf (Italian) parsley leaves
2 garlic cloves, very finely chopped
1 small pickling onion or large French
 shallot, finely chopped
1 thumb-size green chilli, halved,
 seeded, finely chopped
80 ml (2½ fl oz/⅓ cup) extra virgin
 olive oil
1½ tablespoons white wine vinegar

2 CHIMICHURRI SAUCE
PREPARATION: 10 MINUTES • MAKES: 250 ML (9 FL OZ/1 CUP)

Feel free to use your favourite vinegar in this. The important thing is that it's good quality and not too acidic. For white, I like sauvignon blanc or rice wine vinegar. Sherry vinegar is good too, but use a little less as it is strong. If using red vinegar, go for a sweet cabernet sauvignon.

Chop the herbs and put them in a bowl with the garlic, onion and chilli and combine well. Stir in the olive oil and vinegar, then season to taste with salt.

1 small red onion, chopped
1 small handful of coriander (cilantro)
 stems and leaves
125 g (4½ oz) cherry tomatoes (grape
 or pomodorino, if available)
½ red capsicum (pepper)
2 teaspoons tomato paste
 (concentrated purée)
50 ml (1¾ fl oz) extra virgin olive oil
1½ tablespoons red wine vinegar
1½ teaspoons smoked paprika
pinch of sugar

3 SMOKY TOMATO CAPSICUM SALSA
PREPARATION: 10 MINUTES • MAKES: 250 ML (9 FL OZ/1 CUP)

The smoked paprika kicks up this Chilean salsa of chopped tomatoes, capsicum and onion.

Put all the ingredients in a food processor and pulse until roughly chopped. Alternatively, you can chop all the vegetables and herbs by hand. Pour into a bowl and season with salt and freshly ground black pepper to taste.

Quesadillas are a no-brainer when you need to whip up a snack from your fridge: if you have good cheese, a jar of salsa and tortillas you're in business. Anything you add from there is upside: sautéed mushrooms, leftover chicken, roasted poblano chillies or steamed potato. Pickled jalapeños are a powerful ingredient. They instantly perk up a salsa or counter rich ingredients such as crispy chorizo and red Leicester cheese.

CHORIZO, CHEESE & PICKLED JALAPEÑO QUESADILLAS

PREPARATION: 10 MINUTES • COOKING: 15 MINUTES • SERVES: 4–6 AS A SNACK

2 raw chorizo sausages, sliced
  or chopped
3 spring onions (scallions),
  thinly sliced
1½ tablespoons finely chopped
  pickled jalapeño
200 g (7 oz) red Leicester or sharp
  cheddar cheese, grated
small handful of coriander (cilantro)
  leaves, chopped
4 large flour tortillas
1½ tablespoons vegetable oil

Guacamole (see page 68), salsa,
  chipotle Tabasco sauce or other
  hot sauce, to serve

Heat a large frying pan over low heat. Add the chorizo and cook until crisp and most of the fat has been rendered. Remove with a slotted spoon and drain on paper towel.

Put the chorizo, spring onion, pickled jalapeño, cheese and coriander in a bowl and combine well. Divide the mixture between half the tortillas, then top with the remaining tortillas.

Divide the vegetable oil between two frying pans large enough to fit the tortillas and put them over low heat. Alternatively you can cook one at a time. Cook the quesadillas, pressing them flat with a spatula for 5 minutes on one side or until golden and the cheese is melting. Turn and cook the other side until golden, then remove from the pan. Cut each quesadilla into wedges and serve with guacamole, salsa, chipotle Tabasco sauce or other hot sauce.

GET AHEAD Make the quesadillas earlier in the day and stack them, uncooked, on a plate, covered. When ready to serve, heat the pans and cook as above.

In Mexico, street stalls sell these orange-hued pork tacos, slicing the meat off rotating spits. The pork is marinated in achiote (annatto seed paste), pineapple and chilli, giving it the distinct colour and taste. This version doesn't attempt to use a spit but instead does include an ancho chilli and pineapple salsa to produce a close riff on the original. If you haven't made a dried chilli sauce before, I urge you to give it a go. Reconstituted chillies, blackened garlic and onion are puréed with apple cider vinegar and sugar to supply the perfect smoky tang.

TACOS AL PASTOR WITH PINEAPPLE & SMOKY ANCHO CHILLI SALSA

PREPARATION: 15 MINUTES, PLUS 30 MINUTES SOAKING • COOKING: 15 MINUTES • SERVES: 4–6

2 pork fillets, about 450 g (1 lb) each, sinew removed, cut into 2 cm (¾ inch) slices

2 teaspoons vegetable oil

1 small pineapple, peeled, cored, finely chopped

1 red or white onion, finely chopped

½ cup coriander (cilantro) leaves, chopped

flour or corn tortillas, warm, to serve

lime wedges, to serve

Smoky ancho chilli salsa

5 dried ancho chillies

500 ml (17 fl oz/2 cups) boiling water

2 onions, thickly sliced

8 garlic cloves, unpeeled

1½ tablespoons chipotle paste or chipotles in adobo

2 tablespoons chopped coriander (cilantro) leaves

2 tablespoons apple cider vinegar

3 teaspoons soft brown sugar

2 teaspoons salt

To make the salsa, remove the stems and seeds from the dried chillies. Put the chillies in a heatproof bowl, add the boiling water and soak for 30 minutes. Drain and reserve 250 ml (9 fl oz/1 cup) of the water.

Meanwhile, put the onion and garlic in a large heavy-based frying pan over medium heat and dry-fry, shaking the pan frequently, for 10 minutes until blackened. Remove from the pan and, when cool enough to handle, peel the garlic. Put all of the ingredients in a blender with the reserved water and purée until smooth. Check the seasoning and adjust if necessary. Transfer to a small airtight container and refrigerate for up to 2 weeks.

Preheat a barbecue or chargrill pan to medium. Toss the pork slices with 125 ml (4 fl oz/½ cup) of the salsa, then drizzle with the vegetable oil. Cook the pork slices for 2 minutes on each side or until just cooked through. Chop into smaller pieces.

Put the pineapple, onion and coriander in a bowl and toss to combine. Serve the pork with warm tortillas, lime wedges, the remaining salsa and the pineapple salad.

GET AHEAD Grill the pork earlier in the day, then cover and refrigerate. Add more salsa and cover with foil before reheating in a 200°C (400°F) oven for 10 minutes.

My friends call these 'crack enchiladas' for their highly addictive nature. Let's just say you'll be tempted to let out a button or two when you're finished. They're best made on the weekend when you have time to lovingly put them together. Unlike the bloated soggy enchiladas you get in some Mexican restaurants these have crisp corn shells and a mouth-watering tangy red chilli sauce. They're not difficult but it will take a little effort.

ENCHILADAS WITH RED CHILLI SAUCE

PREPARATION: 40 MINUTES • COOKING: 40 MINUTES • SERVES: 4–6

50 ml (1¾ fl oz) vegetable oil
750 g (1 lb 10 oz) boneless, skinless
  chicken thighs
1 red onion, finely chopped
1 handful of coriander (cilantro)
  leaves, coarsely chopped
200 g (7 oz) cheddar cheese, grated
12 corn tortillas

Pickled jalapeños, Escabeche
  (see page 67) and crème fraîche,
  to serve

Red chilli sauce
8 dried guajillo, pasilla or
  ancho chillies
500 ml (17 fl oz/2 cups) boiling water
1 onion, thickly sliced
5 roma (plum) tomatoes, halved
8 garlic cloves, unpeeled
1 teaspoon dried wild oregano
125 ml (4 fl oz/½ cup) cider vinegar
60 g (2¼ oz) soft brown sugar
2 teaspoons salt

To make the red chilli sauce, remove the stems and seeds from the dried chillies. Put them in a frying pan over high heat and dry-fry for 30 seconds on each side or until lightly toasted. Transfer to a heatproof bowl, cover with the boiling water and soak for 30 minutes, then drain.

Meanwhile, preheat a grill (broiler) on high. Line a baking tray with foil and lay the onion and tomatoes, cut-side up, on the tray. Cook under the grill until the top edges are blackened.

Put the garlic cloves in a small frying pan over medium heat and dry-fry, shaking the pan frequently, for 10 minutes or until blackened. Remove from the heat and, when cool enough to handle, peel the garlic.

Put the blackened tomatoes, onion and peeled garlic in a blender. Add the remaining ingredients, including the drained chillies, with 125 ml (4 fl oz/½ cup) water and process until smooth. Check the seasoning and add extra salt, sugar and vinegar if necessary. If you wish, you can push the sauce through a fine sieve to remove the chilli and tomato skins; this isn't usually necessary if the sauce is finely puréed. Blenders will do a better job of this than food processors because they have four blades instead of two.

CONTINUED

ENCHILADAS WITH RED CHILLI SAUCE (CONTINUED)

GET AHEAD The chilli sauce can be made up to 1 week ahead, covered and refrigerated. Cook the chicken and prepare the filling earlier in the day. You can roll and prepare the enchiladas, then cover and refrigerate up to 4 hours before baking.

Heat 1 tablespoon of oil in a large frying pan over medium–high heat. Season the chicken pieces with salt and freshly ground black pepper and cook until browned on both sides. Reduce the heat to low and cook, shaking the pan regularly for 8 minutes or until the chicken is just cooked through. Remove from the pan, allow to cool slightly and cut the chicken into 3 cm (1¼ inch) pieces. Put the pieces in a bowl with the onion, coriander and three-quarters of the grated cheese and combine well.

Preheat the oven to 220°C (425°F) or 200°C (400°F) fan forced.

Pour 250 ml (9 fl oz/1 cup) of the chilli sauce over the base of a large baking dish. Trim 1 cm (½ inch) off the ends of the tortillas (this will help you fit two snug rows of six into the one dish). Microwave or steam the tortillas for a few seconds to soften them, then quickly place a scant ¼ cup of the chicken mixture along the centre of each tortilla. Roll up tightly and place in the dish, seam-side down. Brush the top of the enchiladas with the remaining oil, then scatter with the remaining cheese. Bake for 15 minutes or until the cheese is melted and the tortillas are crisp.

While the enchiladas are baking, lightly heat the remaining chilli sauce. Serve the hot enchiladas immediately with the chilli sauce, sliced pickled jalapeños or escabeche and crème fraîche.

I do love fried fish tacos with their puffy crisp batter but it's the kind of thing you're better off eating out, leaving no lingering fish aromas in your kitchen. Grilled swordfish, marinated in lime, spices and honey makes a healthy and equally delicious option. A fresh mango salsa and chipotle crema tops it off for a sublime taco.

GRILLED SWORDFISH TACOS WITH MANGO SALSA & CHILLI CREMA

PREPARATION: 20 MINUTES, PLUS 30 MINUTES MARINATING • COOKING: 5 MINUTES • SERVES: 4–6

600 g (1 lb 5 oz) skinless swordfish
  steaks, or other firm white fish,
  cut into 3 cm (1¼ inch) cubes
juice and zest of 2 limes
1 tablespoon honey
1 tablespoon vegetable oil
1 teaspoon garlic salt
1 teaspoon mild chilli powder
1 teaspoon ground cumin
1 teaspoon sugar

Corn tortillas, sliced radishes and
  chipotle Tabasco sauce or other
  chilli sauce, to serve

**Mango, green chilli and red
  onion salsa**
1 small red onion, thinly sliced
juice of 1 lime
2 small mangoes, diced
1 thumb-size green chilli, thinly sliced
small handful of chopped coriander
  (cilantro) leaves

Chilli crema
100 g (3½ oz) sour cream
juice of 1 lime
3 teaspoons chipotle Tabasco
  or other hot chilli sauce

Put the fish in a shallow non-metallic dish. Add the lime zest and juice, honey and oil and combine well. Cover and refrigerate for 30 minutes.

Meanwhile, to make the mango salsa, put the onion and lime juice in a small bowl and toss together. Stand for a few minutes, then add the remaining ingredients and season with salt and freshly ground black pepper.

To make the chilli crema, combine all of the ingredients in a small bowl, then season and set aside.

Preheat a barbecue or chargrill pan on medium–high heat. If using wooden skewers, soak them in water for at least 10 minutes to prevent them from burning during cooking. Combine the spices, sugar and a good pinch of salt in a small bowl. Remove the fish from the marinade and pat dry on paper towel. Thread onto the skewers and lay them on a tray, then dust with the spice mix. Cook the fish skewers for 2–3 minutes on both sides or until just cooked through. Serve with warm tortillas, sliced radishes, mango salsa, chilli crema and chilli sauce.

GET AHEAD Chop the components earlier in the day, cover and refrigerate. Marinate the fish for no more than 30 minutes before you grill, otherwise it will 'cook' the fish.

These chicks on sticks are found all over the streets of Peru. They're similar to yakitori, which shows the influence of the Japanese who migrated in the nineteenth century as labourers. Traditionally the marinade uses a paste made from chillies called aji panca (red) or aji amarillo (yellow). Although specialist stores sell them, they can be elusive. A spoonful of fruity hot chilli sauce slots in just fine.

PERUVIAN ANTICUCHOS
PREPARATION: 30 MINUTES, PLUS 1 HOUR MARINATING • COOKING: 10 MINUTES • SERVES: 4–6

500 g (1 lb 2 oz) boneless chicken thighs with skin, halved

Creamy Aji Verde Sauce (see page 52), fruity hot sauce, finely chopped red onion and coriander (cilantro) sprigs, to serve

Marinade
1 thumb-size fresh red chilli
1 garlic clove
juice of ½ lime
3 teaspoons soy sauce
3 teaspoons fruity hot chilli sauce
1½ tablespoons rice wine vinegar
1 teaspoon ground cumin

To make the marinade, finely chop or purée the chilli, garlic and all of the remaining ingredients in a blender, then season with salt and freshly ground black pepper.

Combine the chicken with the marinade in a bowl, then cover and refrigerate for 1 hour or overnight if time permits. If using wooden skewers, soak them in water for at least 10 minutes to prevent them from burning during cooking. Thread the chicken onto the skewers.

Preheat a barbecue or chargrill pan to low. Cook the chicken skewers for 5 minutes on each side or until cooked through. Serve with aji verde sauce, finely chopped red onion and coriander sprigs.

GET AHEAD Marinate the chicken the day before and keep refrigerated. The sauce can be made earlier in the day, covered and refrigerated. Grill just before serving.

Tostadas belong in the taco family but are baked or fried flat instead of folded over. They make a perfect raft for melted cheese, tangy chipotle black beans and shredded chicken. Serve it with a creamy green aji verde sauce and crunchy slaw to bring it all together for a Mexican taste bomb. See front cover of the book for a photograph of this dish.

BLACK BEAN & CHICKEN TOSTADAS

PREPARATION: 30 MINUTES • COOKING: 25 MINUTES • SERVES: 6

vegetable stock (optional)
3 boneless, skinless chicken breasts
200 ml (7 fl oz) Smoky ancho chilli salsa (see page 54, or purchase ready-made)
1 tablespoon vegetable oil
2 garlic cloves, finely chopped
2 x 400 g (14 oz) tins black beans, drained and rinsed
45 ml (1½ fl oz) cider vinegar
2 teaspoons ground cumin
1 tablespoon soft brown sugar
3 teaspoons chipotle purée

Creamy Aji Verde Sauce (see page 52) and Crunchy Slaw (see page 68), to serve
Mexican hot sauce, such as chipotle Tabasco, to serve
2 limes, quartered, to serve

Tostadas
12 fresh corn tortillas
2 tablespoons vegetable oil, for brushing
100 g (3½ oz) sharp white cheddar cheese, grated

Preheat the oven to 190°C (375°F) or 210°C (415°F) fan forced. Bring a saucepan of water or vegetable stock to a boil. Add the chicken breasts and boil for 3 minutes. Remove from the heat and cover with a lid. Allow to stand in the liquid for 20 minutes, then remove the chicken.

Allow the chicken to cool for 10 minutes, then shred and put the meat in a bowl. Pour the Mexican salsa over the chicken and toss together. Season with salt and pepper and transfer to a frying pan to reheat later.

Heat the oil in a large frying pan. Add the garlic and sauté over medium heat for a few minutes until golden. Add the beans and heat through for a few minutes. Add the vinegar, cumin and a good teaspoon of salt. Cook for a further 2 minutes or until the liquid is reduced by half. Add the soft brown sugar and chipotle purée and stir. Let the mixture cook for another 5 minutes and then remove from heat.

Make the tostadas just before eating. Brush both sides of the tortillas with the vegetable oil. Spread them in a single layer on two baking trays. Bake for 7 minutes until golden, then sprinkle the cheese over the tortillas. Cook for another 2 minutes until the cheese is melted.

While the tortillas are cooking, reheat the chicken in a frying pan over low heat until warmed through.

Serve the warm tostadas topped with a big spoonful of beans, chicken, creamy aji verde sauce and the crunchy slaw. Serve Mexican hot sauce separately and provide plenty of napkins.

This delicious stick-to-your-bones feijoada stew is found all over Brazil. The traditional recipe, which originated with Portuguese traders, is full of nose-to-tail piggy ingredients. Offcuts such as ears, tails and trotters get cooked up with black beans for hours. Sometimes you have to take liberties with classics; I took a little detour with my rendition, which features less exotic and fatty meat and a fresh topping of coriander salsa. My talented friend Sarah Cook introduced me to the genius addition of a little cocoa powder which gives a sweet depth of flavour.

BLACK BEAN & PORK STEW

PREPARATION: 15 MINUTES, PLUS OVERNIGHT SOAKING • COOKING: 2½ HOURS • SERVES: 4–6

3 raw chorizo sausages, cut into 5 cm (2 inch) pieces

1 tablespoon olive oil

500 g (1 lb 2 oz) small meaty pork ribs

500 g (1 lb 2 oz) boneless pork shoulder, cut into 5 cm (2 inch) pieces

3 onions, finely chopped

4 garlic cloves, finely chopped

pinch of chilli flakes

250 g (9 oz) dried black beans, soaked overnight

2 bay leaves

1 teaspoon unsweetened cocoa powder

1 teaspoon ground cumin

2 tablespoons white wine vinegar

Steamed rice and hot chilli sauce, to serve

Coriander and onion salsa

2 large handfuls of coriander (cilantro) leaves

1 small white onion

1 thumb-size green chilli, seeded and diced juice of 1 lime

Heat a large heavy-based saucepan with a fitted lid over medium heat. Put in the chorizo and half of the olive oil and cook until the chorizo is golden all over. Remove the chorizo from the pan, leaving as much oil behind as possible, and set aside.

Increase the heat to high and cook the ribs and pork shoulder in batches until golden all over. Remove the meat from the pan and set aside. Reduce the heat to medium, add the remaining oil, onion, garlic and chilli, season with salt and freshly ground black pepper and cook for 7–8 minutes until the onions are soft.

Drain the black beans and add them to the pan, along with the browned pork, ribs and chorizo. Add just enough water to cover—about 650 ml (22½ fl oz)—and the bay leaves, cocoa, cumin and vinegar and bring to the boil. Reduce the heat to low, cover and simmer for 2 hours or until the beans are soft and the meat is tender. During the last hour of cooking, check the stew and, if there is too much liquid, remove the lid for the remaining cooking time. Season with more salt or vinegar if desired.

To make the coriander and onion salsa, put all of the ingredients in a bowl, season and stir to combine well. Serve the feijoada with steamed rice, the coriander and onion salsa and some hot chilli sauce.

GET AHEAD The stew can be made 3 days in advance and stored in the refrigerator. Gently reheat with a little extra water, as it will thicken after refrigeration. You can also freeze this stew. The salsa can be prepared 2–3 hours in advance, covered and refrigerated.

SLOW OR FAST COOKING You can also use a slow cooker set on the short (4-hour) method or make a quick version of the stew using a pressure cooker, cooking in batches for 30 minutes each. Another method is to cook in the oven for 3–4 hours at 160°C (315°F) or 140°C (275°F) fan forced.

Passionfruit are plentiful in Brazil. Called maracujá, it is also the name of this simple mousse pudding. I have taken liberties with the classic recipe and fashioned it into a tray cake with a biscuit base and a little gelatine to hold it together for cutting. This recipe calls for quite a bit of juice, so if you want to make your life easier buy tinned passionfruit juice; just make sure it isn't sweetened. Be sure to buy a few extra fruit, too, as you want a few seeds for crunch. Let the smooth-skinned ones ripen; when they go wrinkly that means they're ready.

PASSIONFRUIT MOUSSE SLICE

PREPARATION: 30 MINUTES, PLUS 3 HOURS SETTING • COOKING: 5 MINUTES • SERVES: 6–8

175 g (6 oz) digestive biscuits
  (graham crackers)
50 g (1¾ oz) unsalted butter, melted
18 passionfruit, plus extra to serve
3 sheets platinum-strength gelatine
600 ml (21 fl oz) sweetened
  condensed milk
300 ml (10½ fl oz) thick (double)
  cream (48% fat), lightly whipped

Fruit coulis
2 ripe mangoes
juice of 1 lime
3 teaspoons caster (superfine) sugar

Grease and line a 20 cm (8 inch) square cake tin with baking paper, leaving the paper overhanging on two sides.

Put the biscuits in a food processor and finely crush. Add the melted butter and combine well. Press the biscuit mixture over the base of the tin and press down firmly. Refrigerate while you make the filling.

Cut the passionfruit in half, then scoop out the flesh into a sieve placed over a bowl. Press down on the seeds with the back of a spoon to extract as much juice as you can. You will need 170 ml (5½ fl oz/⅔cup) of strained juice. Reserve 2 heaped tablespoons of seeds and discard the rest. Put the juice in a small saucepan over low heat and stir until hot.

Soak the gelatine sheets in cold water for 2–3 minutes until soft. Squeeze out the gelatine to remove the excess water, then add to the hot juice and stir until dissolved. Transfer to a large bowl, then add the condensed milk and stir until well combined. Fold in the softly whipped cream until just combined, then pour over the biscuit base in the tin and refrigerate for 3 hours or until set.

Meanwhile, to make the fruit coulis, peel and chop one mango into large pieces and put it in a food processor with the lime juice and sugar. Process until smooth and the sugar is dissolved. Cut the remaining mango into small pieces for serving.

To serve, cut the mousse cake into squares and top each piece with a little fruit coulis, a little mango and a small spoonful of passionfruit seeds.

GET AHEAD The cake can be made in full up to 2 days before, covered and refrigerated.

EXTRAS & SIMPLE SIDES

BAKED TORTILLA CHIPS

PREPARATION: 5 MINUTES • COOKING: 10 MINUTES •
MAKES: 1 LARGE BOWL OF CHIPS (ABOUT 120 PIECES)

These are infinitely better than store bought and if you're going to the trouble of making home-made tacos or guacamole, they only take 10 minutes in the oven. See the photograph on page 42.

10 corn tortillas
vegetable oil, for brushing
sea salt, for sprinkling

Preheat the oven to 210°C (415°F) or 190°C (375°F) fan forced.

Brush the tortillas on both sides with vegetable oil. Use scissors to cut each tortilla into 6 triangles. I stack three or four and slice them together. Spread the triangles in a single layer over two large baking trays and bake for 8–9 minutes until golden and crisp. Remove from the oven and sprinkle with salt.

GET AHEAD You can store the chips for up to 2 days in an airtight container. Reheat in a hot oven for 2 minutes to restore crispness.

GRILLED CORN ON THE COB WITH MAYO, CORIANDER & GRATED CHEESE

PREPARATION: 5 MINUTES • COOKING: 5 MINUTES • SERVES: 6

The perfect side dish for a South American outdoor barbecue. You can cut the cobs in half before cooking if you like. Authentically the cheese used is queso fresco, which is a mild crumbly soft cheese variety. Parmesan works well as a replacement and all the flavours meld together when piping hot.

6 corncobs, husks and silk removed
90 g (3¼ oz) whole-egg mayonnaise
25 g (1 oz/¼ cup) finely grated parmesan cheese
2 tablespoons finely chopped coriander
  (cilantro) leaves
1 lime, cut into small wedges for squeezing

Preheat a barbecue or chargrill pan to high heat.

Cook the corncobs in a large saucepan of boiling water for 5 minutes. Remove the pan from the heat and leave the corn in the water until ready to grill.

Just before serving, remove the corn from the water and pat dry with a clean tea towel (dish towel). Brush all over with mayonnaise and season with salt and freshly ground black pepper. Grill for 5 minutes, turning regularly, until grill marks appear. Sprinkle the corncobs with parmesan and coriander, then serve immediately with lime wedges to squeeze over them when eating.

GET AHEAD Boil the corn up to 1 hour before grilling and keep it in the water. Coat and grill just before serving.

ESCABECHE

PREPARATION: 15 MINUTES • COOKING: 5 MINUTES •
SERVES: 4–6 AS A SNACK OR CONDIMENT

In the scrappy little taco joints of Mexico there is always a bowl of escabeche on every plastic table. Scoop up the pickled slices of carrot and jalapeño with tortilla chips for an amazing snack or use it as a salsa on tacos or enchiladas.

200 ml (7 fl oz) apple cider vinegar
3 teaspoons salt
3 teaspoons sugar
3 teaspoons dried wild oregano
4 carrots, peeled and diced
1 small onion, finely chopped
1 jalapeño or small green chilli, cut into thick slices
2 garlic cloves, halved
1½ tablespoons vegetable oil

Put the vinegar, salt, sugar, oregano and 100 ml (3½ fl oz) water in a saucepan over medium heat and bring to the boil. Put the carrot, onion, chilli, garlic and vegetable oil in a 500 ml (17 fl oz/2 cup) capacity glass jar or sealable container. Pour the hot liquid over the vegetables, seal and stand until cool. Refrigerate overnight, then serve, drained, with tortilla chips.

GET AHEAD Escabeche will keep for up to 1 month or more, when refrigerated in a sealed container.

CRUNCHY SLAW

PREPARATION: 5 MINUTES • SERVES: 6

Whip up this simple topping in just a few minutes.

**2 large handfuls (1 heaped cup) of shredded
  white cabbage**
6 radishes, thinly sliced
**small handful of coriander (cilantro) leaves,
  roughly chopped**
1 thumb-size green chilli, stem removed, sliced

Juice of 1 lime (optional) to serve

Mix all of the ingredients together in a bowl and
serve as a topping for Black Bean & Chicken
Tostadas (see page 60) or add a squeeze of lime
juice and season with salt to serve alongside other
spicy meat dishes.

GUACAMOLE

PREPARATION: 5 MINUTES • SERVES: 4–6 AS A SNACK

**Guacamole is best mashed as the Mexicans do using
the giant stone molcajete mortar and pestles. The
flavours are melded together with all the bashing
and it makes a marked difference to the final taste.
I sometimes use a potato masher or the end of
a rolling pin to improvise.**

1 long green chilli or jalapeño, halved, seeded
½ garlic clove
small handful of coriander (cilantro) leaves
½ small white onion, finely chopped
3 very ripe avocados
juice of 2 limes

Baked Tortilla Chips (see page 66) to serve

Pound the chilli, garlic and coriander in a mortar and
pestle until finely mashed, or finely chop by hand.
Transfer to a bowl and add the onion, avocado and
lime juice and season with salt and freshly ground
black pepper. Mash it all together, then serve with
Baked Tortilla Chips.

GET AHEAD Prepare up to 6 hours ahead and store,
covered, in the refrigerator. Make sure you put plastic
wrap directly onto the surface of the guacamole so it
doesn't discolour.

FLAVOURS OF THE MEDITERRANEAN

AGRODOLCE & PICCANTE

The roasted balsamic onions lend a pickled taste to this bean salad and have a stunning colour. Serve this alongside any grilled meat, chicken or haloumi.

BORLOTTI BEAN & OLIVE SALAD WITH ROASTED BALSAMIC ONIONS

PREPARATION: 20 MINUTES • COOKING: 20 MINUTES • SERVES: 4–6

3 red onions, thickly sliced into rings
pinch of sugar
juice of ½ lemon
80 ml (2½ fl oz/⅓ cup) extra virgin olive oil
60 ml (2 fl oz/¼ cup) balsamic vinegar
100 g (3½ oz) green beans
two 400 g (14 oz) tins of borlotti beans, drained and rinsed
200 g (7 oz) cherry tomatoes, halved
2 celery stalks, thinly sliced, pale leaves reserved
8 mild or oil-cured black olives, pitted
large handful of fresh basil

Preheat the oven to 190°C (375°F) or 170°C (325°F) fan forced.

Spread the onion slices in a single layer on a large baking tray. Season with salt and freshly ground black pepper and sprinkle with the sugar. Drizzle with lemon juice, a little of the olive oil and half the balsamic vinegar. Roast for 20 minutes or until just tender and crisp at the edges.

Meanwhile cook the green beans in a saucepan of salted boiling water for 2 minutes. Drain, then refresh under cold running water. Pat dry with a clean tea towel (dish towel).

To serve, place the borlotti beans on a platter and top with the tomato, celery, celery leaves, green beans, olives, onion and all of the juices and the basil leaves. Drizzle with the remaining olive oil and balsamic vinegar, toss gently and serve immediately.

GET AHEAD All of the components for the salad can be prepared earlier in the day, but wait to combine until just before serving.

Everyone adores a juicy meatball and that's why practically every country has its own version. It has to be said that this recipe is basically Italian but hugely influenced by the Americans. The Southern Italian immigrants who moved to America at the turn of the century took liberties with the 'polpetta' (Italian for meatball) and morphed it into spaghetti and meatballs. Italians don't usually eat them with pasta: they are more of a snack or a dish on their own.

PORK MEATBALLS WITH ASIAGO, LEMON & PARSLEY

PREPARATION: 30 MINUTES • COOKING: 30 MINUTES • SERVES: 4–6

100 g (3½ oz/1⅔ cups) fresh fine
   breadcrumbs
125 ml (4 fl oz/½ cup) milk
500 g (1 lb 2 oz) minced (ground) pork
4 slices prosciutto, finely chopped
60 g (2¼ oz) asiago, pecorino or
   parmesan cheese, grated
finely grated zest of 1 lemon
2 garlic cloves, crushed
¼ teaspoon fennel seeds,
   coarsely ground
1 teaspoon chilli flakes
1 teaspoon dried oregano
1 teaspoon salt
¼ cup finely chopped flat-leaf
   (Italian) parsley, plus extra to serve
60 ml (2 fl oz/¼ cup) olive oil

Line a baking tray with baking paper. Put the breadcrumbs and milk in a large bowl and soak for a few minutes. Add all of the remaining ingredients except the oil and use your hands to combine well. Wash your hands, then rub them with a little oil: this will keep the mixture from sticking while you roll. Roll the mixture into golf-ball size pieces and place on the prepared tray.

To cook the meatballs, you can pan-fry or bake them.
To pan-fry, heat the oil in a large heavy-based frying pan over medium–high heat and cook the meatballs in batches until they are golden all over. Drain on paper towel. Don't try to turn the meatballs if they are sticking: sometimes they just need more time to brown and then release themselves.

To bake the meatballs, preheat the oven to 220°C (425°F) or 200°C (400°F) fan forced. Drizzle the meatballs on the tray with the oil and roll them around on the tray to coat. Bake for 15 minutes or until golden and cooked through, shaking the tray halfway through cooking. Both methods produce great results but the pan-fried is a bit browner. Serve the meatballs with toothpicks and a little more chopped parsley sprinkled over them.

GET AHEAD Make the meatballs, place them on the tray and keep covered and refrigerated for up to 2 days. You can also brown the outside of the meatballs, undercooking the centre, then cover and refrigerate. To finish, preheat the oven to 200°C (400°F) or 180°C (350°F) fan forced. Transfer the meatballs to a large roasting pan, cover with foil and bake for 5 minutes or until cooked through.

When making grilled meat or pizza you need a good tossed salad to go alongside and this is the one. Peppery rocket and bitter radicchio are tossed with pear, fennel and a sharp sherry vinaigrette. Little taste pops of sultanas, parmesan and toasted almonds appear in every forkful for a truly delicious salad.

FENNEL, PEAR & RADICCHIO SALAD WITH MARCONA ALMONDS & SHERRY VINAIGRETTE

PREPARATION: 15 MINUTES • SERVES: 4

¼ head of radicchio, outer leaves
  discarded, roughly chopped
1 firm ripe pear, halved, cored,
  cut into 3 cm (1¼ inch) pieces
1 fennel bulb, halved, cored, cut
  into 3 cm (1¼ inch) pieces
2 large handfuls of wild rocket
  (arugula)
2 slices sourdough bread, toasted
  and cut into cubes
30 g (1 oz) parmesan cheese, shaved
55 g (2 oz/⅓ cup) Marcona or regular
  almonds, toasted
45 g (1½ oz /¼ cup) sultanas
  (golden raisins)

Dressing
1 French shallot, finely chopped
3 teaspoons sherry vinegar
50 ml (1¾ fl oz) extra virgin
  olive oil
1 teaspoon dijon mustard
pinch of sugar

Place all of the salad ingredients in a large bowl. If you're making the salad ahead of time, rub the pear pieces with lemon to prevent them browning.

To make the dressing, combine all of the ingredients in a jar and season with salt and freshly ground black pepper. Seal and shake well. Pour over the salad and serve immediately.

GET AHEAD Make the dressing and chop all the ingredients for the salad except the pear earlier in the day. Prepare the pear and toss all of the ingredients together just before serving.

The two seasons of artichokes, spring and autumn, are wholeheartedly embraced in Southern Italy. Romans bathe them in a sauce of lemon and mint, the Neapolitans fry them and in Sardinia they're even pickled. The preparation can be a purgatorial task so it's a vegetable to relish. The baby ones don't take much peeling so they are much easier. For me, frying is more the exception than the rule, but it's one of the best ways to eat these.

CRISP ARTICHOKE FRITTERS WITH LEMON SAFFRON AÏOLI

PREPARATION: 20 MINUTES • COOKING: 10 MINUTES • SERVES: 4–6

10 baby globe artichokes
2 lemons, halved
150 g (5½ oz/1 cup) plain (all-purpose) flour
3 eggs, lightly beaten
150 g (5½ oz/2½ cups) panko (Japanese) breadcrumbs
light olive oil, for frying

Lemon saffron aïoli
½ garlic clove, crushed with 1 teaspoon salt
1 egg yolk, at room temperature
2 teaspoons dijon mustard
pinch of saffron threads
60 ml (2 fl oz/¼ cup) light olive oil or sunflower oil
juice of ½ lemon

To make the aïoli, put the crushed garlic, egg yolk, mustard and saffron in a bowl and whisk together until well combined. Whisking constantly, gradually add the oil, drop by drop at first and then in a slow steady stream until the mixture is thick and emulsified. Add the lemon juice and season to taste with salt.

To clean the artichokes, snap off the outer leaves and discard. Use a small paring knife to cut along the outer perimeter, removing more leaves. Chop off the top third and discard. Use a vegetable peeler to remove the outer layer of the stem and the sides of the artichoke. Slice in half lengthways and, if there is any furry choke inside, use a teaspoon to remove it. Put the peeled artichokes in a large bowl of cold water with the lemons squeezed in to prevent the artichokes from oxidising.

Put the flour, eggs and breadcrumbs into three separate shallow bowls. Drain the artichokes and pat them dry with a clean tea towel (dish towel). Dust the artichokes with flour and shake off the excess, then dip them into the beaten egg and coat in the breadcrumbs.

Heat a wok or heavy-based saucepan with 5 cm (2 inches) of the light olive oil over medium heat. When a piece of bread dropped into the oil sizzles instantly, the oil is ready. Deep-fry the crumbed artichokes, about 4 at a time, for 2 minutes each or until golden brown. Drain on paper towel and serve warm on a board or platter, with the lemon saffron aïoli.

GET AHEAD The baby artichokes can be cleaned and crumbed earlier in the day. Place them in a single layer on a tray lined with baking paper. Cover with plastic wrap and refrigerate until needed. The aïoli can be prepared the day before, then covered and refrigerated.

There's one word to describe this homage to tomatoes: sublime. If you've ever been to Greece, then you are likely to have come across these tomato fritters. They make them on many of the islands, but they originate from Santorini. I first tasted them in Crete and have never forgotten them. A thick batter of tomatoes, mint and flour is dropped into hot olive oil, fried crisp and then eaten with lemon wedges and cold dill yoghurt. Baby plum tomatoes are best but you can also use large ripe ones if you remove the seeds.

SANTORINI TOMATO FRITTERS WITH YOGHURT

PREPARATION: 15 MINUTES • COOKING: 15 MINUTES • SERVES: 4–6

400 g (14 oz) ripe roma (plum) or pomodorino (baby plum) tomatoes
1½ tablespoons chopped mint
1 teaspoon dried oregano
90 g (3¼ oz) plain (all-purpose) flour
1 teaspoon baking powder
1 teaspoon salt
light olive oil, for pan-frying
250 g (9 oz) Greek-style yoghurt
1 tablespoon finely chopped dill
lemon wedges, to serve

Cut the tomatoes in half lengthways, scoop out and discard the seeds, then dice the flesh. If using baby tomatoes, cut them lengthways into quarters and leave the seeds in. Combine the tomato flesh, mint, oregano, flour, baking powder and salt in a medium bowl with 80 ml (2½ fl oz/⅓ cup) of water and stir until a thick batter forms.

Heat 5 cm (2 inches) of oil in a wok or medium heavy-based saucepan over medium–high heat. When a piece of bread dropped into the oil sizzles quickly, the oil is ready. Using a lightly oiled soup spoon, carefully drop large tablespoons of the batter into the oil—about 4 at a time—and cook them for 30–40 seconds on each side until golden and crisp. Drain on paper towel.

Combine the yoghurt and dill in a small bowl and serve with the hot fritters and lemon wedges.

GET AHEAD The tomatoes can be chopped, covered and refrigerated earlier on the day of making, but the batter needs to be mixed together just before frying.

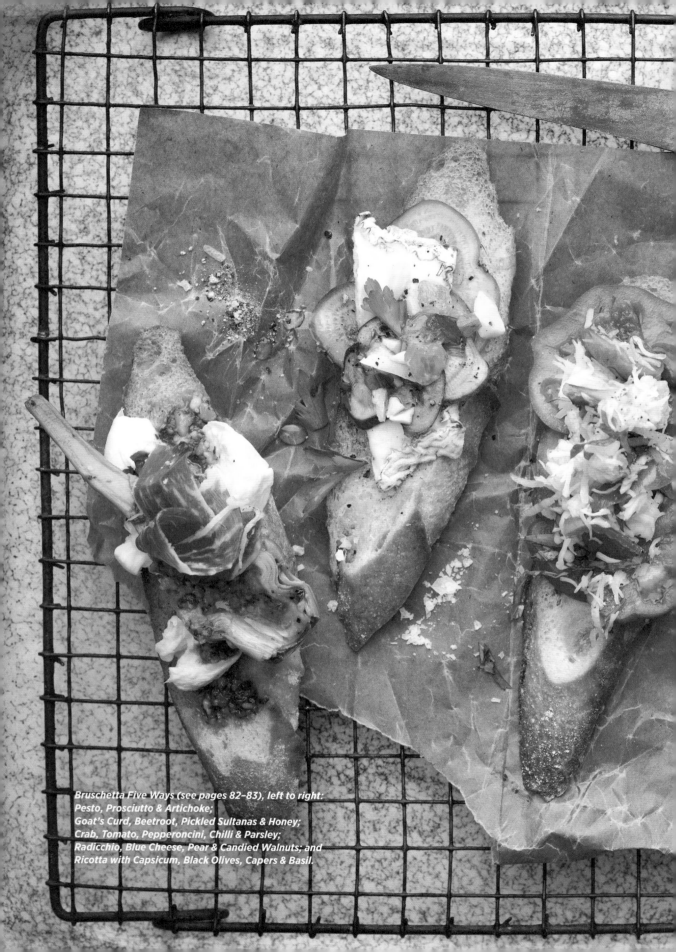

Bruschetta Five Ways (see pages 82–83), left to right:
Pesto, Prosciutto & Artichoke;
Goat's Curd, Beetroot, Pickled Sultanas & Honey;
Crab, Tomato, Pepperoncini, Chilli & Parsley;
Radicchio, Blue Cheese, Pear & Candied Walnuts; and
Ricotta with Capsicum, Black Olives, Capers & Basil.

Bruschetta, crostini: what's the difference? Technically crostini are 'little toasts' made for canapés; bruschetta is more substantial: grilled bread rubbed with garlic and olive oil. This recipe is for the latter and you can make it as simple as you like—but bring on the quality. The bread is key: sourdough, a country artisan loaf or a traditional French baguette are my favourites, toasting up nicely but staying chewy in the middle. For toppings I like a mix of tastes: pops of saltiness (prosciutto or olives), sour elements (pickled shallots, capers, a drizzle of vinegar) or sweet (sultanas or honey). Finish it off with some crisp breadcrumbs or nuts for a bit of crunch.

BRUSCHETTA FIVE WAYS
PREPARATION: 30 MINUTES • COOKING: 5 MINUTES • SERVES: 4–6

6 slices sourdough bread or
    good quality French baguette
1 garlic clove, bruised
2 tablespoons extra virgin
    olive oil

Toast the bread in your toaster for about 2 minutes or until just golden and still chewy in the middle. Rub lightly on one side with raw garlic, then brush with olive oil. Top with any of the following combinations.

1 GOAT'S CURD, BEETROOT, PICKLED SULTANAS & HONEY
Put 2 tablespoons sultanas (golden raisins) and 2 tablespoons white vinegar in a small saucepan over low heat until warm. Remove from the heat and stand for 5 minutes. Spread the bruschetta with goat's curd or soft goat's cheese, then top each piece with 2 slices cooked golden or red beetroot. Drizzle with extra virgin olive oil and honey, then sprinkle with Marcona almonds (or other toasted almonds) and the pickled sultanas.

2 RADICCHIO, BLUE CHEESE, PEAR & CANDIED WALNUTS
Put 1 tablespoon each of honey, caster (superfine) sugar and olive oil in a small saucepan over medium heat. Stir for 3–4 minutes or until the sugar has lightly caramelised. Stir in 40 g (1½ oz/⅓ cup) of toasted walnuts, combine well, then spread on a piece of baking paper. Top the bruschetta with a thin slice of Dolcelatte (gorgonzola dolce), then add a few slices of pear, a little chopped radicchio and the candied walnuts. Drizzle with honey and season with freshly ground black pepper.

CRAB, TOMATO, PEPPERONCINI, CHILLI & PARSLEY

Combine 1 tablespoon each of white balsamic vinegar and extra virgin olive oil, 1 small finely chopped French shallot and the finely grated zest of 1 lemon to make a vinaigrette. Season with salt and freshly ground black pepper to taste. Top the bruschetta with a couple of slices of ripe oxheart (beefsteak), zebra or delicious tomato, then a spoonful of fresh white crab meat. Drizzle with a little of the vinaigrette, scatter with finely chopped red chilli, chopped parsley and a few pepperoncini (pickled Tuscan pepper).

PESTO, PROSCIUTTO & ARTICHOKE

Spread the bruschetta with good quality pesto. I like to add a little white balsamic vinegar to the pesto to make it tastier. Top with a piece of artichoke preserved in oil and a slice of prosciutto or fennel seed salami.

RICOTTA WITH CAPSICUM, BLACK OLIVES, CAPERS & BASIL

Combine 1 large roasted, peeled, seeded and chopped red capsicum (pepper) with 1 tablespoon of extra virgin olive oil and 1 teaspoon of red wine vinegar. Add 1 teaspoon of capers, 4 halved black olives and a small handful of chopped basil. Spread the bruschetta with fresh ricotta, then top with a little of the capsicum mixture.

GET AHEAD The base for the bruschetta can be cut, toasted and dressed with the garlic and olive oil earlier in the day, sealed in a tin or an airtight plastic container. Add the cheeses and topping no more than 1 hour before serving.

In Madrid and many regions of Spain you take your pick of the tantalising plates packed along the bar to devour with an aperitif. Pintxos, a Basque specialty, translates as 'spike' or skewer. The flavour of Iberian pork is off the charts because of the animals' acorn diet: you can taste a sweet nuttiness in the meat that's unforgettable. I've tried many methods of making crisp pork belly, but getting the crackling crisp was always a gamble until one of my fellow teachers at Leiths School of Food and Wine, Andrea Hamilton, gave me the definitive method: drying the skin by leaving it uncovered in the refrigerator overnight before scoring it and adding salt. After a blast of high heat, it is slow cooked for hours and then blasted once more at the end, then the grand finale is the Spanish quince and sherry vinegar glaze.

BASQUE PORK BELLY PINTXOS WITH SHERRY VINEGAR & QUINCE GLAZE

PREPARATION: 15 MINUTES, PLUS OVERNIGHT MARINATING • COOKING: 3 HOURS • SERVES: 6 AS PART OF A TAPAS, OR 6 AS A MAIN COURSE WITH SALAD

1 teaspoon cumin seeds
1 teaspoon fennel seeds
1 teaspoon smoked paprika
2 kg (4 lb 8 oz) pork belly
  with rind
3 teaspoons sea salt

Quince and sherry vinegar glaze
1 tablespoon olive oil
2 garlic cloves, finely chopped
75 g (2¾ oz) dulce de membrillo
  (quince paste)
125 ml (4 fl oz/½ cup) sherry vinegar
75 g (2¾ oz) soft brown sugar
1 teaspoon chilli flakes

Preheat the oven to 240°C (475°F) or 220°C (425°F) fan forced.

Combine the cumin seeds, fennel seeds and paprika in a mortar and pestle and coarsely grind them, then rub the meat side of the pork belly with the spices. Leave it skin-side up and uncovered in the refrigerator overnight. Place the meat, skin-side up, in a shallow roasting tin. Pat the skin dry using paper towel, then use a sharp knife to score the skin, making sure you don't cut all the way through to the meat. Sprinkle the skin with the sea salt, then roast on the middle shelf of the oven for 30 minutes. Reduce the oven temperature to 160°C (315°F) or 140°C (275°F) fan forced and cook for another 2 hours or until the meat is tender. Increase the oven temperature to 220°C (425°F) or 200°C (400°F) fan forced and cook for another 30 minutes or until the crackling is puffed and crisp.

Meanwhile, to make the glaze, heat the oil in a small saucepan over low heat. Add the garlic and stir for 2 minutes until light golden. Add the dulce de membrillo and stir until melted, then add the vinegar and simmer for 2 minutes or until reduced. Add the sugar, chilli flakes, a pinch of salt and 125 ml (4 fl oz/½ cup) of water. Simmer for another 5 minutes until syrupy, then remove from the heat.

Chop the pork belly into small squares and arrange on a platter. Drizzle with the glaze and serve with toothpicks or, for a more substantial meal, with cooked puy lentils or beans and Fennel, Pear & Radicchio Salad (see page 75).

GET AHEAD The glaze can be made earlier in the day and reheated just before serving.

White Pizza with Broccolini,
Fontina & Sausage
(see pages 88–89)

I got hooked on making pizza after sampling the famous bubbly crusts in Napoli. The Neapolitans are the godfathers of pizza, producing crisp but chewy dough and quality toppings. I've tried all kinds of methods, a bit of sourdough starter, same day rising and even the 'no-stir' dough but I think this is ultimately the best way. The dough uses only a tiny amount of dried yeast and can be used the same day or left to rise for 1–2 days in the refrigerator. The slower it rises, the more flavour and bubbles you'll get. A sprinkling of polenta or semolina on your baking tray lets it slide into the oven and adds another layer of texture. You don't need a five-star oven or a special pizza oven, just good dough.

NAPOLI-STYLE PIZZA

PREPARATION: 15 MINUTES, PLUS AT LEAST 2 HOURS PROVING • COOKING: 10 MINUTES • MAKES: 4 PIZZAS

BASIC PIZZA BASE

Pizza dough
½ teaspoon dried active yeast
  (not fast-acting)
350 ml (12 fl oz) warm water
500 g (1 lb 2 oz/3⅓ cups) 00 (pastry)
  flour, plus extra for dusting
1 teaspoon salt
olive oil, for greasing

Combine the yeast and water in a small bowl and stand for 5–10 minutes or until foamy. This is important because it means the yeast is working. If it doesn't foam, throw it out and start again.

Put the flour and salt into the bowl of an electric mixer fitted with the dough hook. With the mixer on low speed, gradually add the yeast mixture and knead until the dough comes together into a ball and pulls away from the bowl. If necessary, add a little extra flour. Continue to knead with the dough hook for 5–7 minutes or until the dough is smooth and elastic. Lightly rub your hands and a bowl with olive oil. Shape the dough into a ball, transfer it to the bowl and turn to coat lightly in the oil, then cover with plastic wrap and refrigerate for up to 2 days. If you want to use it on the same day then leave it in a warm place to double in size: this is called proving.

If you've refrigerated the dough, take out the portion you want about 2–4 hours before using and let it double in size at room temperature. When you make the pizzas, knock back the dough and knead for another minute. Divide the dough into 4 pieces.

TIP The temperature of your kitchen will determine how quickly the dough rises. During the summer it may only take a couple of hours but in the winter it may take 4–5 hours. If you have a cold draughty kitchen, turn on the oven for 1 minute, turn it off and put the bowl with the dough inside to rise.

WHITE PIZZA WITH BROCCOLINI, FONTINA & SAUSAGE

1 quantity proved pizza dough,
at room temperature
semolina, polenta or flour, for dusting
1 tablespoon olive oil
250 g (9 oz) Italian sausage, casings
removed, meat pinched into 3 cm
(1¼ inch) pieces
1 bunch broccolini (baby broccoli),
trimmed
150 g (5½ oz) fontina, provolone
piccante or asiago cheese,
thinly sliced
125 g (4½ oz) fresh mozzarella,
drained, torn into pieces
1 large garlic clove, thinly sliced
1 teaspoon chilli flakes

GET AHEAD Make the dough 1–2 days ahead, and keep it covered and refrigerated in an oiled bowl. Toppings such as broccolini can be blanched earlier in the day, refreshed and refrigerated.

Preheat your oven to the highest temperature it will go (not fan forced) and place a pizza stone or a large metal baking tray on the middle rack. Use another baking tray covered with polenta, semolina or flour as a 'pizza peel'. This acts as the 'wheels' to allow the pizza to slide onto the heated stone or metal tray.

To prepare the toppings, heat the olive oil in a non-stick frying pan over medium heat. Cook the sausage meat until lightly browned, then remove from the pan and set aside.

Meanwhile, cook the broccolini in a large saucepan of lightly salted water for 1 minute. Drain and refresh under cold water.

Divide the dough into 4 pieces and keep 3 covered with a clean tea towel (dish towel) while you make the first pizza. Don't use a rolling pin to stretch the dough, only your fingers, thus ensuring the bubbles don't get pressed out. If your dough is at room temperature it will stretch easily. Stretch the dough out on a work surface lightly dusted with flour into a 25 cm (10 inch) round, making sure the dough can move easily over the surface without sticking.

Transfer the stretched dough to the prepared pizza peel and scatter with one-quarter of each of the toppings: the sausage, broccolini, fontina and mozzarella cheese, garlic slices and chilli flakes. Slide onto the preheated pizza stone or hot baking tray and cook for 4–5 minutes or until crisp on the bottom.

If the oven is hotter at the back, turn the pizza halfway through cooking. Meanwhile, prepare the next pizza for cooking. Remove the cooked pizza from the oven and immediately pop the next one in.

Variations

To make a calzone, place the filling on one side of the stretched or rolled dough. Brush the edges with a little water and fold the dough over. Turn the edges over to seal like an empanada. Cut a small hole in the top for the steam to escape, then slide onto the preheated stone or tray and cook for 7–8 minutes.

Other combinations

· garlic oil with burrata, sliced tomato, basil and rocket (arugula)
· artichoke, salami, pepperoncini (pickled Tuscan pepper) slices, crushed tinned tomatoes and fontina cheese
· Italian pork meatballs, mozzarella, crushed tinned tomatoes, garlic and basil
· mixed wild and brown mushroom slices, sage and mozzarella

Chorizo makes everything taste good and that's a fact. The paprika oil infuses everything with garlic smokiness and this prawn tapas is no exception. I ate this in Barcelona and nearly licked my plate. The lemon cuts through the rich prawns and salty salami. Eat with crusty bread so you don't miss out on the sauce.

PRAWNS WITH CHORIZO, CHILLI, LEMON & PARSLEY

PREPARATION: 10 MINUTES • COOKING: 5 MINUTES • SERVES: 4 AS A STARTER

150 g (5½ oz) raw chorizo sausages,
  cut into 1 cm (⅜ inch) slices
1 tablespoon extra virgin olive oil
2 garlic cloves, thinly sliced
400 g (14 oz) large raw prawns,
  butterflied
1 teaspoon chilli flakes
juice and finely grated zest of 1 lemon
2 tablespoons finely chopped
  flat-leaf (Italian) parsley

Crusty bread and chargrilled lemon
  halves, to serve

Heat a large frying pan over medium heat. Add the chorizo and cook for 3–4 minutes or until crisp and the oil is released. Remove from the pan and discard most of the oil. Add the olive oil to the pan and reduce the heat to medium–low. Cook the garlic for 1 minute or until just starting to colour.

Increase the heat to high, then add the prawns and chilli flakes and toss for 1 minute. Add the lemon juice and chorizo and toss for another minute or until the prawns are opaque. Sprinkle the zest and parsley over the prawns and serve immediately with crusty bread and chargrilled lemon halves.

GET AHEAD Crisp the chorizo earlier in the day, cover and refrigerate. Everything else can be quickly pan-fried just before serving.

Chunks of swordfish are marinated in vinegar, wild oregano and garlic and then grilled for a Greek feast. You can wrap it up in soft flatbread with cucumber yoghurt or eat it on its own with rice. It makes a lighter change from lamb yiros (kebab), but if you still fancy red meat you can use the same marinade and sauce.

SOUVLAKI-STYLE SWORDFISH WITH TZATZIKI

PREPARATION: 10 MINUTES, PLUS 30 MINUTES MARINATING • COOKING: 10 MINUTES • SERVES: 4

750 g (1 lb 10 oz) skinless swordfish, cut into 4 cm (1½ inch) cubes
60 ml (2 fl oz/¼ cup) extra virgin olive oil, plus extra, to drizzle
juice and finely grated zest of 1 lemon
3 teaspoons dried wild oregano
1 garlic clove, crushed
1½ tablespoons cabernet sauvignon red wine vinegar

Warm pitta bread, chopped cos (romaine) lettuce and halved cherry tomatoes, to serve

Tzatziki
2 Lebanese (short) cucumbers, grated
1 garlic clove, crushed
250 g (9 oz) Greek-style yoghurt
1 tablespoon finely chopped dill

If using wooden skewers, soak them in water for 30 minutes to prevent them from burning during cooking. Put the fish in a non-metallic dish with the olive oil, lemon juice and zest, oregano, garlic and vinegar. Season to taste and combine well. Cover and refrigerate for 30 minutes.

Meanwhile, to make the tzatziki, put the grated cucumber in a clean tea towel (dish towel) and squeeze out all the excess liquid. Put it in a bowl with the remaining ingredients, season to taste and combine well. Refrigerate until serving.

Heat a barbecue or chargrill pan to medium–high heat. Remove the fish from the marinade, drain and pat dry using paper towel. Thread onto the skewers, then drizzle with the extra oil. Grill for 2–3 minutes each side or until dark grill marks appear. Serve the fish wrapped in warm pitta bread, topped with chopped lettuce, tomatoes and a spoonful of the tzatziki.

GET AHEAD The fish can be sliced, the marinade mixed and tzatziki made earlier in the day. Don't marinate the swordfish until about 30 minutes before grilling so it doesn't 'cook' through too much and dry out.

Oregano grows wild all over the countryside in Sicily and Calabria. The Sicilians make judicious use of it with salmoriglio sauce. The word means 'to brine' and it is used to marinate fish, pork or lamb or just served as a sauce. You can either barbecue skewers or prepare this as a whole butterflied leg of lamb. The longer you leave it to marinate the better, overnight if possible.

SALMORIGLIO LAMB SKEWERS WITH CAPER MINT SAUCE

PREPARATION: 15 MINUTES, PLUS AT LEAST 2 HOURS MARINATING • COOKING: 20 MINUTES • SERVES: 4–6

1.5 kg (3 lb 5 oz) boneless leg
  of lamb, butterflied
3 teaspoons chilli flakes
5 garlic cloves, smashed
2 heaped tablespoons soft
  brown sugar
50 ml (1¾ fl oz) extra virgin olive oil
15 g (½ oz) oregano leaves,
  finely chopped
juice and finely grated zest of 1 lemon

Borlotti Bean & Olive Salad (see
  page 73) or simmered puy lentils
  (or tiny blue-green lentils), to serve

Caper mint sauce
¼ cup flat-leaf (Italian) parsley
¼ cup mint leaves
1 anchovy, rinsed
1 garlic clove, finely chopped
3 teaspoons tiny capers in brine,
  drained
3 teaspoons sherry or red wine
  vinegar
80 ml (2½ fl oz/⅓ cup) extra virgin
  olive oil
large pinch of chilli flakes

Season the lamb all over with salt and freshly ground black pepper. Cut the lamb into 5 cm (2 inch) pieces and place in a glass or ceramic dish.

Combine the remaining ingredients in a small bowl, then pour over the lamb and massage the marinade into the meat. Cover and stand for 2 hours or refrigerate overnight if time permits. Bring back to room temperature before grilling. If using wooden skewers, soak them in water for 30 minutes to prevent them from burning during cooking. Thread the meat onto the skewers.

Meanwhile, to make the caper mint sauce, finely chop all the herbs, anchovy, garlic and capers and combine them in a small bowl. Add the vinegar and oil, season to taste with salt, pepper and chilli flakes, and set aside.

Light a charcoal grill and allow the coals to die down to a pinkish-grey colour. Use indirect heat to let the lamb cook slowly without burning, by placing a drip pan between the coals and the grill. If using gas, turn off the middle heat source so that there is no heat directly below the meat. Cook for 4 minutes each side. Loosely cover the lamb with foil and rest for 10 minutes, then serve with the caper mint sauce, Borlotti Bean & Olive Salad or simmered lentils.

GET AHEAD Marinate the meat the night before cooking, cover and refrigerate. Prepare the caper mint sauce about 2 hours before eating. Herbs are best chopped closer to serving to keep their colour.

Sicilians are the masters when it comes to the 'agrodolce': sweet and sour. This peasant-style chicken is brimming with that vibe and more. Serve it up over pasta, rice or a good mash.

SICILIAN VINEGAR CHICKEN

PREPARATION: 20 MINUTES • COOKING: 1 HOUR 10 MINUTES • SERVES: 4–6

6 corn-fed, free-range chicken
  Marylands (leg quarters)
plain (all-purpose) flour, for dusting
60 ml (2 fl oz/¼ cup) extra virgin
  olive oil
1 large onion, halved and sliced into
  half moons
3 garlic cloves, finely chopped
2 celery stalks, diced
125 ml (4 fl oz/½ cup) red wine
  vinegar
1 teaspoon chilli flakes
1 tablespoon tomato paste
  (concentrated purée)
250 ml (9 fl oz/1 cup) white wine
125 ml (4 fl oz/½ cup) chicken stock
3 teaspoons tiny capers in brine,
  drained
45 g (1½ oz/¼ cup) sultanas
  (golden raisins)
pinch of sugar
2 tablespoons finely chopped
  flat-leaf (Italian) parsley

Season the chicken with salt and freshly ground black pepper, then dust with flour and shake off the excess.

Heat 1 tablespoon of the oil in a large heavy-based saucepan with a fitted lid over medium heat. Cook the chicken until browned all over, then remove from the pan and set aside. Add the remaining oil, the onion, garlic and celery and season to taste. Cook, stirring, for 10 minutes or until soft.

Add the vinegar and simmer for 2–3 minutes, then add all of the remaining ingredients except the parsley and return the chicken pieces to the pan. Season with a little more salt and pepper, then cover and reduce the heat to low: simmer gently for 40 minutes or until the chicken is tender. Remove the lid and simmer for another 10 minutes or until the sauce is slightly thickened and reduced. Alternatively you can bake the chicken at 190°C (375°F) or 170°C (325°F) fan forced for 1 hour, removing the lid in the last 10 minutes. Sprinkle with parsley and serve with pasta, mash or rice.

GET AHEAD The entire dish can be made 1 day ahead, cooled, then covered and refrigerated. Reheat over low heat until the chicken is warmed through.

If you adore pulled pork then you will fall hopelessly in love with porchetta. Pork shoulder is rolled in a thick crust of spices and herbs and slow roasted until it falls apart. My Italian mother made it when I was growing up, but her version was very different from what I experienced in Rome. While meandering through the tiny alleyways of the Trastevere I followed the breeze of garlic and bought a crusty pork-filled roll from a street vendor. Traditionally it is prepared with a whole deboned pig stuffed with wild herbs, loads of garlic, and roasted with the crackling skin. Authenticity isn't always practical, so let's go with Mama's recipe: it's better and miles easier.

ROMAN PORCHETTA SANDWICHES

PREPARATION: 15 MINUTES • COOKING: 5 HOURS • SERVES: 6

2 kg (4 lb 8 oz) boneless pork shoulder, rind removed, rolled and tied with string

4 garlic cloves, cut into slivers

60 ml (2 fl oz/¼ cup) olive oil

1½ tablespoons fennel seeds

1½ tablespoons dried oregano

1½ tablespoons finely chopped rosemary

3 teaspoons chilli flakes

3 teaspoons sea salt

3 teaspoons freshly ground black pepper

Sprigs of fresh herbs, crusty rolls and rocket (arugula), to serve

Preheat the oven to 160°C (315°F) or 140°C (275°F) fan forced.

Using a sharp knife, make small incisions in the meat and insert the slivers of garlic into the holes. Rub the meat with 1 tablespoon olive oil and season with salt and freshly ground black pepper all over. Heat a very large frying pan over high heat and cook the meat until browned on all sides. Remove from the pan, then rub the remaining oil over the pork.

Combine the fennel seeds, oregano, rosemary, chilli flakes, sea salt and black pepper on a plate. Roll the seared meat in the herb and spice mixture and place it on a roasting rack in a roasting pan. Bake for 4–5 hours or until the meat is very tender and falls apart when the string is removed.

Slice the pork and place it on a platter with rosemary sprigs and other fresh herbs. Serve with crusty rolls and rocket for guests to assemble their own.

GET AHEAD The pork can be studded with garlic and rolled in the spices and herbs the night before, then covered and refrigerated. You can roast it earlier in the day and reheat the meat, covered in foil, in a 180°C (350°F) fan forced oven to serve.

Children will be disappointed when they find out these ice-cream sandwiches have coffee in them, but that's all the more for us adults to indulge in with this outrageous trio of chewy almond meringues, coffee ice cream (buy a good quality tub or make your own) and thick milk chocolate fudge sauce.

COCOA & ALMOND MERINGUES WITH FUDGE SAUCE & COFFEE ICE CREAM

PREPARATION: 20 MINUTES, PLUS 2 HOURS COOLING • COOKING: 35 MINUTES • MAKES: 8

3 eggwhites, at room temperature
180 g (6¼ oz) caster (superfine) sugar
1 teaspoon white wine vinegar
50 g (1¾ oz) blanched almonds, toasted, finely chopped
3 teaspoons unsweetened cocoa powder

Coffee ice cream
1 tablespoon instant espresso coffee powder
500 ml (17 fl oz/2 cups) vanilla ice cream, left to soften slightly

Chocolate fudge sauce
100 g (3½ oz) dark chocolate (70% cocoa), chopped
150 ml (5 fl oz) thick (double) cream
30 g (1 oz) unsalted butter
80 ml (2½ fl oz/⅓ cup) golden syrup (light corn syrup)
100 g (3½ oz) caster (superfine) sugar
1 teaspoon natural vanilla extract

GET AHEAD Make the sandwiches in full up to 3 days ahead. Store in the freezer in a covered container until ready to serve.

Preheat the oven to 170°C (325°F) or 150°C (300°F) fan forced. Line two baking trays with baking paper.

It is very important to have a spotlessly clean bowl to start so wash the bowl in hot water and dry well. Using an electric mixer fitted with the whisk attachment, whisk the eggwhite until soft peaks form. Start adding the sugar, one tablespoon at a time, until it is all incorporated and the whites are glossy and stiff. Gently fold in the vinegar until just combined. Use a spatula to fold through half of the almonds and half of the cocoa so the mixture has a swirled appearance.

Make 16 individual slightly flattened meringues by spooning tablespoon-size dollops of the mixture onto the prepared trays, leaving 5 cm (2 inches) between each one. Sprinkle with the remaining almonds and cocoa. Turn the oven down to 140°C (275°F) or 120°C (250°F) fan forced. Bake for 35 minutes, then turn the oven off and leave the meringues in the oven for 2 hours: this will help them stay chewy and not hard.

To make the coffee ice cream, line a 20 x 30 cm (8 x 12 inch) tin with baking paper. Put the coffee and 1 tablespoon of the ice cream in a large bowl and stir until dissolved. Add the remaining ice cream and stir until well combined. Spread the ice cream out in the prepared tin, smooth the top and return to the freezer until you are ready to make the sandwiches.

Meanwhile, to make the chocolate fudge sauce, put the chocolate, cream and butter in a heatproof bowl over a saucepan of just simmering water, making sure the base of the bowl doesn't touch the water. Stir until melted, then add the golden syrup, sugar and vanilla. When nearly boiling (still over the saucepan) turn the heat down to low and simmer for 5 minutes or until the sauce is thick. Remove from the heat and set aside to cool.

Spread the flat side of the meringues with a good couple of teaspoons of chocolate sauce. Use a knife or pastry cutter to cut out circles of ice cream and sandwich between 2 meringues. Return to the freezer until firm again.

TOMATO, CAPSICUM & FETA SALAD
WITH OREGANO CROUTONS

PREPARATION: 20 MINUTES • COOKING: 10 MINUTES • SERVES: 4–6

A celebration of all things Mediterranean.

4 large red capsicums (peppers), quartered,
   membranes and seeds discarded
2 slices sourdough bread, chopped into tiny cubes
1½ tablespoons extra virgin olive oil
3 teaspoons dried wild oregano
250 g (9 oz) cherry tomatoes, halved
3 teaspoons tiny capers in brine, drained
3 teaspoons fresh oregano leaves
50 g (1¾ oz) feta cheese, crumbled

Dressing
1½ tablespoons extra virgin olive oil
1 garlic clove, crushed
50 ml (1¾ fl oz) red wine vinegar
1½ tablespoons honey

Preheat the oven grill or broiler to medium–high.
Place the capsicum, skin-side up on a baking tray and
grill for 8–10 minutes until blistered and blackened.
Put the capsicum in a bowl, cover with plastic wrap
and set aside until cool enough to handle. Peel, then
cut into small pieces.

Meanwhile, preheat the oven to 210°C (415°F)
or 190°C (375°F) fan forced. Spread the sourdough
cubes on a baking tray, drizzle with half the olive oil,
then sprinkle with the dried oregano and season with
salt and freshly ground black pepper. Toss to combine,
then bake for 8 minutes until golden and crisp.
Remove and set aside.

To make the dressing, combine all of the
ingredients in a jar with a fitted lid. Season with
salt and pepper, seal and shake well.

To serve, combine the capsicum, tomato, capers
and fresh oregano leaves in a bowl. Pour the dressing
over and toss to combine. Scatter with the feta and
croutons. Serve immediately.

GET AHEAD Prepare the dressing, peppers and
croutons earlier in the day. Assemble the dish
just before serving.

TOMATO & BURRATA SALAD WITH LEMON BREADCRUMBS

PREPARATION: 15 MINUTES • COOKING: 10 MINUTES • SERVES: 4–6 AS A SIDE

All the best flavours of Italy come together for a 'buonissima' salad. Try using white balsamic vinegar instead of the regular variety: it's sweeter and not quite as acidic. Burrata is made from the scraps of mozzarella. It's mixed with cream and then wrapped in mozzarella casing. Put it on your 'food of the gods' list.

50 g (1¾ oz) fresh sourdough breadcrumbs
1 garlic clove, finely chopped
60 ml (2 fl oz/¼ cup) extra virgin olive oil, plus extra for grilling
finely grated zest of 1 lemon
2 French shallots, thinly sliced
1½ tablespoons white balsamic vinegar
4–5 mixed heirloom tomatoes, such as green, zebra, yellow or red oxheart (beefsteak), sliced
1 ball burrata cheese, drained and kept whole
1 handful of basil leaves, finely shredded

Preheat the oven to 210°C (415°F) or 190°C (375°F) fan forced.

Toss the breadcrumbs in a bowl with half the garlic and 1½ tablespoons of the olive oil. Season with salt and freshly ground black pepper. Spread the breadcrumbs on a baking tray and toast for 6 minutes or until golden and crisp. Set aside to cool, then add the lemon zest.

Put the shallots and balsamic vinegar in a small bowl and stand for 5 minutes. Add the remaining oil and season with salt and pepper.

To serve, place the sliced tomatoes on a platter along with the ball of burrata. Pour the dressing over the top, scatter with the basil and crisp breadcrumbs and serve immediately.

GET AHEAD The breadcrumbs (minus the lemon zest) can be made a day ahead and stored in a covered container. Assemble the rest of the salad just before serving.

MIDDLE EASTERN CUISINE

A SPOONFUL OF ALEPPO PEPPER

Filo pastry pies are the Middle East's ultimate snack on the go. Each country makes its own special filling: a medley of cheese, spinach or minced meat. This is my own version with roasted spiced pumpkin, salty feta and toasted pine nuts for bite.

PUMPKIN & FETA TRIANGLES WITH MINT DIPPING SAUCE

PREPARATION: 30 MINUTES • COOKING: 45 MINUTES • MAKES: 27 TRIANGLES

1 small butternut pumpkin (squash), peeled, halved, seeded
2 teaspoons ras-el-hanout or za'atar spice mix
2 tablespoons olive oil
1 large red onion, halved and sliced into half moons
2 garlic cloves, chopped
50 g (1¾ oz/⅓ cup) pine nuts, toasted
50 g (1¾ oz) feta cheese, crumbled
18 sheets filo pastry, 20 x 30 cm (8 x 12 inch) size
melted butter, for brushing
black onion seeds or sesame seeds

Mint sauce
2 large handfuls of mint leaves, coarsely chopped
2 tablespoons caster (superfine) sugar
2 large pinches of chilli flakes, such as Aleppo pepper
2 tablespoons mild white wine vinegar
2 tablespoons extra virgin olive oil

Preheat the oven to 220°C (425°F) or 200°C (400°F) fan forced. Chop the pumpkin into small pieces and put it in a roasting tin. Add the spice mix and 1 tablespoon of the oil and season well with salt and freshly ground black pepper. Roast for 15 minutes or until tender.

Heat the remaining oil in a large frying pan over medium heat. Add the onion and garlic, season with salt and pepper and cook for 10 minutes or until soft. Add the pumpkin and toss for 2–3 minutes, then remove the mixture from the pan and set aside until cool. Add the pine nuts and feta to the cooled pumpkin and combine well.

Put a large baking tray in the oven to heat. Line another tray with baking paper and set it aside.

Lay out 2 sheets of filo pastry at a time and brush the top sheet with melted butter: I find one sheet is too thin, so doubling up keeps it tight. Cut the pastry lengthways into 3 strips. Place a heaped teaspoon of the pumpkin filling in the lower corner of one of the strips. Fold over and up and repeat the folding until you have used the whole strip to form a tight little triangle. Brush again with melted butter, sprinkle with black onion seeds and place on the prepared tray lined with baking paper. Repeat with the remaining pastry sheets and filling.

Transfer the triangles to the preheated baking tray and bake for 15 minutes or until golden brown. Preheating the tray will get the bottom of the pastry crisp.

While the triangles are baking, combine all the ingredients for the mint sauce in a bowl. Season with salt and pepper and serve with the hot triangles.

GET AHEAD The pastries can be made the night before or earlier in the day and stored in the refrigerator on a tray between two sheets of baking paper, covered with plastic wrap. The mint sauce can be prepared up to 3 hours before serving.

Several countries lay claim to inventing falafel, and the various sauces are equally delicious. Lebanon uses a garlic mayonnaise and Israel is partial to sesame tahini. I've chosen the latter and pimped it up with some pickled cabbage for added crunch. Use fresh Middle Eastern flatbread and give it a little heat first to soften while rolling up. If you have time, make my Grilled Flatbread recipe (see page 131). Roll up the warm falafel balls in the soft smoky bread with all the fixings for a little slice of heaven.

FALAFEL WITH LEMON TAHINI & PICKLED CABBAGE
PREPARATION: 35 MINUTES, PLUS OVERNIGHT SOAKING • COOKING: 15 MINUTES • SERVES: 4–6

175 g (6 oz) dried chickpeas, soaked overnight in cold water

1 small onion, coarsely chopped

2 garlic cloves

1 teaspoon ground cumin

1 teaspoon ground coriander

1 handful each of flat-leaf (Italian) parsley leaves and coriander (cilantro) leaves

1 teaspoon baking powder

2 teaspoons salt

2½ tablespoons plain flour

zest of 1 lemon

1½ tablespoons sesame seeds

olive oil, for frying

Flatbread, pieces of pickle, pickled long green chillies, chopped cucumber, tomato, red onion, parsley and mint, to serve

Pickled red cabbage

¼ head red cabbage

3 teaspoons salt

125 ml (4 fl oz/½ cup) apple cider vinegar or white wine vinegar

Lemon tahini sauce

1½ tablespoons tahini

juice and finely grated zest of 1 lemon

½ garlic clove, crushed

50 ml (1¾ fl oz) extra virgin olive oil

1½ tablespoons plain yoghurt

To make the pickled red cabbage, thickly shred the cabbage and toss in a large bowl with the salt. Leave to sit a few hours, then rinse the salt off, drain well and return to the bowl. Pour the vinegar over, cover and refrigerate for at least 2 hours or overnight. Drain before using.

Meanwhile, to make the tahini sauce, whisk the tahini and 1½ tablespoons of water in a bowl until smooth. Add the lemon juice and zest, garlic, olive oil and yoghurt, season with salt and pepper and combine well. Refrigerate until serving.

To make the falafel, drain the chickpeas and put them in a food processor with all of the ingredients except the sesame seeds and olive oil. Process until a thick dough forms. Using lightly floured hands, form the mixture into spheres the size of a ping-pong ball. Put the sesame seeds on a plate, then roll the falafel in the seeds, pressing to coat well.

Heat the oil in a wok or small heavy-based saucepan to about 7 cm (2¾ inches) deep. When a piece of bread dropped into the oil sizzles instantly, the oil is ready. Fry the falafel balls, in batches, until golden brown and drain on paper towel. Serve with warm flatbread, tahini sauce, pickled cabbage and all the accompaniments.

GET AHEAD The pickled cabbage can be made 2–3 days ahead, covered and refrigerated. The falafel can be rolled and refrigerated between sheets of baking paper on a tray, covered with plastic wrap. The tahini sauce can be made earlier in the day. For falafel served at room temperature, they can be fried earlier in the day, covered and refrigerated.

I can't decide which part of this dish I like best: the tender fragrant chicken or the tangy pomegranate salad. This Lebanese dish is characteristic of their healthy captivating food. The amount of chilli flakes might sound enormous but if you're using Aleppo pepper they are truly mild (honestly) and contribute a smoky essence. If using regular chilli flakes, reduce the amount to three teaspoons.

SPICE-CRUSTED CHICKEN WITH POMEGRANATE SALAD

PREPARATION: 20 MINUTES • COOKING: 30 MINUTES • SERVES: 4

750 g (1 lb 10 oz) boneless, skinless chicken thighs
1 tablespoon olive oil
1½ tablespoons Aleppo pepper
1½ tablespoons sumac
1 teaspoon ground cinnamon
1 teaspoon cumin seeds
2 garlic cloves, finely chopped
finely grated zest of 2 lemons
2 tablespoons pine nuts

Rice Vermicelli Pilaff (see page 130), to serve
Greek-style yoghurt, to serve

Pomegranate salad
seeds of 1 pomegranate
1 small onion, halved and sliced into half moons
1 cup flat-leaf (Italian) parsley leaves
1 teaspoon sumac

Preheat the oven to 210°C (415°F) or 190°C (375°F) fan forced.

Put the chicken, olive oil, spices, garlic and lemon zest in a bowl. Season the chicken well with salt and freshly ground black pepper, then spread the pieces out on a baking tray and roast for 25–30 minutes until the chicken is cooked and golden at the edges. During the last 7 minutes of cooking, scatter the pine nuts over the chicken.

To make the pomegranate salad, toss all of the ingredients together. Serve the chicken with the pomegranate salad, Rice Vermicelli Pilaff and a good dollop of yoghurt.

NOTE Aleppo pepper is also known as pul biber or Turkish chilli flakes. See page 51 for more information.

GET AHEAD Season the chicken earlier in the day, cover and refrigerate. The pilaff can be prepared up to the point of adding stock and covered. The ingredients for the pomegranate salad can be chopped but keep them separate until just before serving. Soak the onion in salted iced water and refrigerate to keep it from becoming too odorous. Roast the chicken and finish off the rice just before serving.

I met my friends Seniz and Lihong when taking Italian classes. We spent more time discussing food than we did honing our language skills, so it's no surprise I never became fluent. Seniz is Turkish and a particularly gifted cook. She treated us to a triumphant meze lunch that included this salad and I was fortunate that she shared her recipe with me. Black-eyed peas aren't something I wax lyrical about, but the pomegranate dressing, fresh dill and crisp pickled vegetables will make you rethink this lonely legume.

BLACK-EYED PEA SALAD WITH DILL, PICKLED PEPPERS & POMEGRANATE MOLASSES

PREPARATION: 20 MINUTES, PLUS OVERNIGHT SOAKING • COOKING: 30 MINUTES • SERVES: 4–6

150 g (5½ oz/¾ cup) dried black-eyed peas, soaked overnight in cold water

100 ml (3½ fl oz) pomegranate molasses

6 spring onions (scallions), thinly sliced

60 ml (2 fl oz/¼ cup) extra virgin olive oil

1½ tablespoons finely chopped dill

2 small gherkins (pickles), finely chopped

10 pickled sweet Peppadew® peppers, chopped (see note)

1 large carrot, peeled, finely chopped

1 large handful of shredded white cabbage

POMEGRANATE MOLASSES

Sticky and purple, this syrup closely resembles molasses, but is actually pure pomegranate juice boiled until it is syrupy. Used all over the Middle East, this viscous, sour ingredient is used to great effect for grilled meats, dressings, soups and stews.

Drain the black-eyed peas and put them in a saucepan with enough cold water to cover well. Bring to the boil over medium heat, then simmer for 30 minutes or until tender but not mushy. If you don't have time to soak them overnight, you can bring the unsoaked peas to the boil, then turn off the heat and leave them for 1 hour in the warm water. Drain, then cover with fresh water and cook as for the soaked peas.

Drain the cooked peas and put them in a bowl with half the pomegranate molasses and a little salt. Stand for 10 minutes to allow the pomegranate molasses to soak in, then add all of the remaining ingredients, season with salt and pepper and toss to combine well. Drizzle with the remaining pomegranate molasses and serve. This salad will keep for 3–4 days in the refrigerator.

NOTE You can use pickled sweet Peppadew® peppers or substitute 2–3 pepperoncini (pickled Tuscan peppers).

GET AHEAD The salad can be made in full, covered and refrigerated up to 3 days before. You may need to drizzle with more pomegranate molasses just before serving, as the beans soak up the liquid.

Eggplant is a true chameleon, constantly adapting to different flavours. Spices transform its bland constitution and the texture alters radically depending on whether you grill, fry or roast it. You're always told to remove the water from eggplant before frying and many recipes advise salting to weep the juices out. Well, my advice is the exact opposite. These eggplants soak in water (my mother taught me that trick) to keep them plump while frying, resulting in supremely crisp, spiced-crusted nibbles.

FRIED EGGPLANT STICKS WITH SUMAC & HONEY

PREPARATION: 20 MINUTES, PLUS 1 HOUR SOAKING • COOKING: 30 MINUTES • MAKES: 20–30 STICKS

2 medium eggplants (aubergines)

125 g (4½ oz) plain (all-purpose) flour

2 teaspoons sumac

2 teaspoons za'atar

2 teaspoons garlic salt

1 litre (35 fl oz/4 cups) vegetable or olive oil, for frying

honey, for drizzling

2 tablespoons finely chopped flat-leaf (Italian) parsley

lemon wedges, to serve

ZA'ATAR

Za'atar is a dried spice mix made of sumac, dried wild thyme, toasted sesame seeds, oregano and salt. Sour-tasting sumac adds punch and the herbs impart a woodsy fragrance. Use it on roasted vegetables, grilled chicken and on flatbread with olive oil.

Cut the tops off the eggplants and cut them lengthways into 2 cm (¾ inch) slices. Cut each slice into 2 cm (¾ inch) wide sticks. Submerge the sticks in a large bowl of cold water and soak for 1 hour.

Combine the flour and spices in a shallow bowl.

Heat the olive oil in a wok or heavy-based saucepan over medium heat. The oil will be hot enough if a small piece of eggplant sizzles instantly when dropped in. Take the eggplant sticks directly from the water and dip each one thoroughly in the flour mixture, coating well. Shake off the excess flour and fry 4–6 sticks at a time for 3–4 minutes until golden brown. Drain on paper towel and sprinkle with salt.

Arrange the eggplant sticks on a platter, drizzle with honey and scatter with parsley. Serve immediately with lemon wedges.

GET AHEAD Soak the eggplant the night before, in the refrigerator. Fry just before serving.

Turkish Gozleme with Minced Lamb (see page 114).

Gozleme might sound like a creature from *The Lord of the Rings*, but it's actually a crisp Turkish parcel filled with treasures of meat, onions and spices. When I first tasted these on the streets of Istanbul it was a revelation. The soft dough is pan-fried in olive oil, which creates a chewy golden crust.

TURKISH GOZLEME WITH MINCED LAMB

PREPARATION: 35 MINUTES, PLUS 2 HOURS PROVING • COOKING: 25 MINUTES • SERVES: 4

1 teaspoon dried yeast
1 teaspoon sugar
175 ml (5½ fl oz/⅔ cup) warm water
250 g (9 oz /1⅔ cups) plain
   (all-purpose) flour or strong flour,
   plus extra for kneading and rolling
1 teaspoon salt
olive oil, for frying

Greek-style yoghurt and Pomegranate
   salad (see page 108), to serve

Filling
1 tablespoon olive oil
500 g (1 lb 2 oz) lean minced
   (ground) lamb
2 garlic cloves, finely chopped
2 teaspoons ground cumin
2 teaspoons Aleppo pepper
1 teaspoon ground cinnamon
finely grated zest of 1 lemon
2½ tablespoons sultanas
   (golden raisins)
1 tablespoon tomato paste
   (concentrated purée)
2 tablespoons chopped flat-leaf
   (Italian) parsley
50 g (1¾ oz/⅓ cup) pine nuts, toasted

Combine the yeast, sugar and water in a small bowl and stand for 5–10 minutes or until foamy. This is important because it means the yeast is working. If it doesn't foam, throw it out and start again.

Put the flour and salt in the bowl of an electric mixer fitted with the dough hook and mix on low speed. Add the yeast mixture and mix until the dough comes together into a ball. If the dough is still sticking to the bowl then add a couple of tablespoons of flour to allow it to come free. Knead in the electric mixer for 10 minutes or until smooth and elastic. (Alternatively, the dough may be mixed by hand in a bowl and kneaded on a floured work surface.)

Transfer to a lightly oiled bowl, turn to coat, then cover with plastic wrap and stand in a warm place for 2 hours or until doubled in size.

Meanwhile, to make the filling, heat half the oil in a large frying pan over high heat. When the pan is really hot, add the lamb and cook for 5 minutes, breaking up any lumps with a spoon. Season well with salt and freshly ground black pepper, pour off the excess fat and transfer to a bowl. Add the remaining oil and the garlic to the pan and cook for 1 minute or until golden. Return the lamb to the pan, add the spices, lemon zest, sultanas, tomato paste and 1 tablespoon water and combine well. Pour the filling onto a tray and stand until cool. Add the parsley and pine nuts, check the seasoning and combine well.

The filling can be made the day before, covered and refrigerated. The dough can be made up to 2 days before and refrigerated (if you do this, reduce the amount of yeast to ½ teaspoon). Take the dough out to come to room temperature 3 hours before using. You can make the parcels 2 hours ahead, and store them on trays between layers of baking paper, covered with plastic wrap. Grill or pan fry just before serving.

When the dough is ready, divide it into 6 portions. Roll out each portion on a lightly floured surface into a 16 cm (6¼ inch) square. Spoon a quarter of the filling onto the bottom half of each square, leaving a 2 cm (¾ inch) border around the edges. Bring the top half of the dough over to enclose the filling, pinch the sides together and twist over to seal.

Heat two large frying pans over medium heat. Drizzle a little oil into the pans and, when hot, add 1 or 2 gozleme (depending on how big your frying pans are) and cook for 4 minutes on each side or until golden and crisp. Serve the hot gozleme with yoghurt and a drizzle of pomegranate molasses.

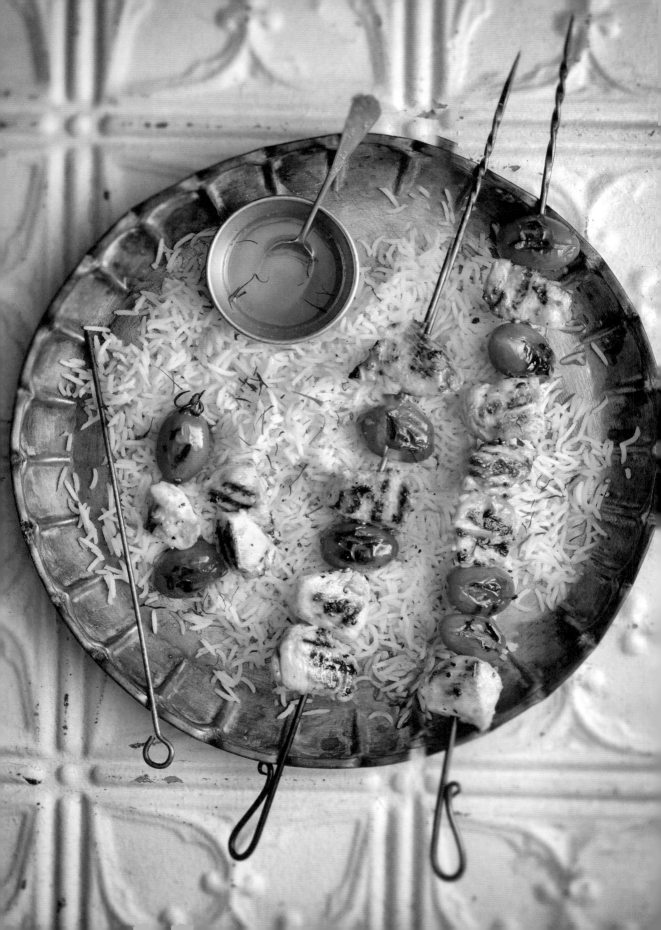

Jujeh kabab—Iranian chicken skewers—are a simple but mesmerising dish with saffron garlic butter. Cherry tomatoes are added to keep it fresh. Eat them with the traditional saffron rice pilaff or wrap in warm flatbread with yoghurt and herbs.

SAFFRON CHICKEN & CHERRY TOMATO KEBABS
PREPARATION: 15 MINUTES, PLUS 1 HOUR MARINATING • COOKING: 10 MINUTES • SERVES: 4–6

4–6 boneless, skinless chicken
  breasts
1 onion, grated
finely grated zest and juice of
  2 lemons
1 teaspoon chilli flakes or Aleppo
  pepper
2 tablespoons extra virgin olive oil
1 heaped teaspoon saffron threads
45 g (1½ oz) butter, melted
1 garlic clove, crushed
250 g (9 oz) large cherry tomatoes

Grilled Flatbread (see page 131) or
  Saffron rice pilaff (see page 130),
  to serve

Cut the chicken breasts into 4 cm (1½ inch) pieces and put them in a non-metallic bowl. Add the onion, lemon zest, half the lemon juice, the chilli flakes and olive oil.

Put the saffron threads in a small bowl and crush them with the end of a knife or rolling pin. Pour 1 teaspoon of boiling water over the threads and stand for 1 minute to infuse. Add half the saffron mixture to the chicken, season with salt and freshly ground black pepper and massage the marinade into the flesh. Cover and refrigerate for 1 hour or overnight if time permits. Add the melted butter and garlic to the bowl with the remaining saffron and combine well. Set aside for cooking.

If using wooden skewers, soak them in water for at least 10 minutes to prevent them from burning during cooking. Just before cooking, thread the chicken and tomatoes onto skewers.

Preheat a barbecue or chargrill pan to medium heat. Brush the chicken skewers with the saffron butter and grill for 2–3 minutes on each side. Keep brushing with the saffron butter to keep them moist. Serve the chicken and tomato skewers with Saffron Rice Pilaff or wrap in warm flatbread.

GET AHEAD The chicken can be marinated the night before and brought to room temperature before grilling. It cooks fast so it's best to grill just before serving.

Dips are a linchpin in the meze composition and warm, soft flatbread is an essential accompaniment. See page 131 for my home-made Grilled Flatbread recipe.

THREE DIPS FOR GRILLED FLATBREAD

4 very ripe tomatoes, seeded, roughly chopped

2 teaspoons tomato paste (concentrated purée)

1 small red onion, diced

3 teaspoons sumac

3 teaspoons Aleppo pepper

juice of 1 lemon

30 ml (1 fl oz) extra virgin olive oil

2 tablespoons chopped flat-leaf (Italian) parsley

2 tablespoons chopped coriander (cilantro) leaves

Grilled Flatbread (see page 131), to serve

1 TOMATO, ALEPPO PEPPER & PARSLEY DIP
PREPARATION: 10 MINUTES • SERVES: 4

Use your end-of-summer glut of tomatoes to create this fresh Turkish tomato dip. The beautiful smoky Aleppo pepper really makes this, but if you can't get hold of it use 1 teaspoon of crushed red chilli flakes instead.

Put all of the ingredients in a bowl, season with salt and freshly ground black pepper and toss to combine well. Serve with warm Grilled Flatbread.

NOTE Aleppo pepper is also known as pul biber or Turkish chilli flakes. See page 51 for more information.

GET AHEAD Chop the ingredients earlier in the day, but keep them separate. Soak the onion in salted iced water or simply chop at the last minute. Combine the ingredients just before serving.

CONTINUED

Three Dips for Grilled Flatbread, clockwise from top: Spiced Feta Dip (see page 120); Yemeni Green Chilli Dip with Yoghurt (see page 120); and Tomato, Aleppo Pepper & Parsley Dip (opposite).

100 g (3½ oz) shanklish, feta or firm
goat's cheese, crumbled
½ small red onion, finely chopped
2 roma (plum) tomatoes, seeded,
chopped
2 tablespoons diced red capsicum
(pepper)
1 tablespoon chopped mint
1 teaspoon sumac
1 teaspoon za'atar or ground cumin
60 ml (2 fl oz/¼ cup) extra virgin
olive oil

Grilled Flatbread (see page 131),
to serve

SPICED FETA DIP
PREPARATION: 10 MINUTES • SERVES: 4

Shanklish, a spice-crusted, tennis ball-size sheep's cheese, is a Syrian and Lebanese specialty. Crumbled and tossed with olive oil and herbs, it's wonderful scooped up in warm flatbread. You can get it from Middle Eastern shops or substitute feta or goat's cheese.

Combine all of the ingredients in a bowl and season with salt and freshly ground black pepper. Toss to mix well, then serve on a platter or in a shallow bowl and eat with warm flatbread.

GET AHEAD You can make the dip without the olive oil 2 hours ahead, then cover and refrigerate. Bring it to room temperature and add the olive oil just before serving.

250 g (9 oz) Greek-style yoghurt
1 tablespoon extra virgin olive oil

Grilled Flatbread (see page 131),
to serve

Zhug
1 garlic clove
2 thumb-size green chillies, seeded
½ small white onion, chopped
2 teaspoons white wine vinegar
or sherry vinegar
1 teaspoon ground cumin
1 large handful of coriander (cilantro)
leaves, coarsely chopped
1 large handful of flat-leaf (Italian)
parsley, coarsely chopped
1 teaspoon salt
2 tablespoons extra virgin olive oil

YEMENI GREEN CHILLI DIP WITH YOGHURT
PREPARATION: 10 MINUTES • SERVES: 4

Zhug, a fiery green chilli herb sauce, originated from Yemen but is used all over the Middle East to spoon over falafel, swirl into dips or serve alongside grilled kebabs. This recipe makes about three times the quantity of zhug you will use to make the dip, but the sauce will keep, refrigerated, for over a month.

To make the zhug, put all of the ingredients in a food processor and process until chopped, but not too fine.
Spread the yoghurt onto a flat plate. Drizzle with the olive oil and swirl a good spoonful of the zhug into the middle. Store the remainder in the refrigerator. Serve with warm flatbread.

GET AHEAD The zhug can be made up to 1 month ahead. Store in a screw-top jar with the top covered in extra virgin olive oil. Don't add to the yoghurt until near serving.

Put your ripe summer tomatoes to good use and make this refreshing Persian salad, from the city of Shirazi. Chopped tomatoes, cucumbers and onions are tossed with a sharp lime dressing and a burst of fragrant herbs. Use a combination of tomato varieties such as mini roma (plum), oxheart (beefsteak), green zebra and vine-ripened. Serve up a beautiful platter of this alongside grilled skewers or any Middle Eastern dish.

PERSIAN TOMATO SALAD

PREPARATION: 15 MINUTES • SERVES: 4–6

500 g (1 lb 2 oz) mixed heirloom
  tomatoes
3 Lebanese (short) cucumbers,
  roughly peeled, halved, sliced
4 radishes, trimmed, thinly sliced
4 spring onions (scallions),
  thinly sliced
1 tablespoon roughly chopped dill
1 tablespoon snipped chives
1 handful of flat-leaf (Italian) parsley
1 handful of mint leaves

Dressing
1 garlic clove, mashed with 1 teaspoon
  salt
juice of 1 lime
2 teaspoons red wine vinegar
50 ml (1¾ fl oz) extra virgin olive oil

Slice or cut the tomatoes in different ways: cut thick slices from the big ones, halve the small ones and cut the vine-ripened tomatoes in quarters, for example, so that there is a mixture of shapes and sizes. Arrange the tomatoes on a platter or in a shallow bowl with the cucumber, radish, spring onion and herbs.

Combine all of the ingredients for the dressing in a glass jar with a fitted lid. Season with salt and pepper, then shake well. Pour over the salad and toss gently.

GET AHEAD Chop all of the ingredients and make the dressing earlier in the day, but don't combine and toss until just before serving.

Nuts are enshrined in Middle Eastern cooking: rolled into buttery pastry, salted for meze, chopped into dips or scattered over salads. This emerald green dressing is made with rich pistachios and sour chopped lemon. Even if you don't like beetroot, you can use this umami sauce on other vegetables, grilled meat or chicken. I love baby beetroot in all the beautiful colours of red, yellow and candy stripe. Farmers' markets usually have the best selection.

ROASTED BEETROOT WITH PISTACHIO & LEMON HERB DRESSING

PREPARATION: 20 MINUTES • COOKING: 1 HOUR • SERVES: 4–6

6–8 yellow or purple beetroot (beets)
2 tablespoons olive oil

Dressing
1½ tablespoons white wine vinegar
60 ml (2 fl oz/¼ cup) extra virgin
 olive oil
1 garlic clove, finely chopped
20 g (½ oz) pistachio nut kernels,
 toasted, finely chopped
1 teaspoon caster (superfine) sugar
1 tablespoon finely chopped chives
1 lemon, peel and pith removed, flesh
 segmented and finely chopped

Preheat the oven to 220°C (425°F) or 200°C (400°F) fan forced.

Lay the beetroot on a double layer of foil, drizzle with the oil and season with salt. Wrap up into a sealed parcel with plenty of room for air to circulate. Roast for 40–60 minutes or until tender. The time will vary depending on how large your beetroot are. You can also steam the beetroot, sprinkled with salt, for 30–40 minutes. Cool slightly, then use paper towel to rub off the skin. Slice in half. They look nice with the tops on but you can remove them if you like. Put them in a shallow bowl.

Combine all of the ingredients for the dressing in a small bowl. Season with salt and freshly ground black pepper to taste and whisk until well mixed. Pour the dressing over the warm beetroot to serve.

GET AHEAD The dressing can be made earlier in the day, but leave the garlic out until close to serving. Roast or steam the beetroot up to 4 hours ahead, peel, and drizzle with some vinegar, olive oil and salt to keep juicy. Slice the beetroot and dress the salad just before serving.

Turkish pizzas, known as 'pide', are topped with mouth-watering toppings such as salty haloumi, spiced lamb and tomato sauce or simply fresh spices and oil. Minced (ground) lamb is used, but finely chopped leg meat is even better. Leftover roast lamb also works beautifully and is even easier.

SPICY LAMB PIZZA

PREPARATION: 40 MINUTES, PLUS 2 HOURS PROVING • COOKING: 25 MINUTES • MAKES: 4 PIZZAS

1 teaspoon dried yeast
350 ml (12 fl oz) warm water
500 g (1 lb 2 oz/3⅓ cups) plain
    (all-purpose) flour or strong flour,
    plus extra for dusting
1 teaspoon salt
semolina, for dusting

Combine the yeast and water in a small bowl and stand for 5–10 minutes or until foamy. This is important because it means the yeast is working. If it doesn't foam, throw it out and start again.

Put the flour and salt in the bowl of an electric mixer fitted with the dough hook and mix on low speed. Add the yeast mixture and mix until the dough comes together into a ball. If the bottom is still sticking then add a couple of tablespoons of flour to allow it to come free. Knead in the mixer for 8–10 minutes or until smooth and elastic. (Alternatively, the dough may be mixed by hand in a bowl and kneaded on a floured work surface.)

Transfer the dough to a lightly oiled bowl, turn to coat, then cover with plastic wrap and stand in a warm place for 2–4 hours until doubled in size. If your kitchen is cold, turn your oven on for a minute and then turn it off and put the dough inside to rise. You can also put it in the refrigerator overnight, punch it down and allow it to rise again at room temperature.

Meanwhile, to make the lamb topping, heat the olive oil in a large frying pan over medium–high heat until hot. Add the onion and garlic and cook for 5 minutes or until golden. Add the lamb and cook for 5 minutes or until brown, breaking up any lumps with a spoon. Pour off excess oil. Add the spices, tomato paste and the pomegranate molasses, season with salt and freshly ground black pepper and cook for another minute. Remove from the heat and cool.

Spicy lamb topping
1 teaspoon olive oil
1 onion, finely chopped
2 garlic cloves, finely chopped
500 g (1 lb 2 oz) lean lamb leg meat, finely chopped, or minced (ground) lamb
2 teaspoons ground cumin
2 teaspoons ground cinnamon
1½ tablespoons Aleppo pepper or 3 teaspoons chilli flakes
1½ tablespoons tomato paste (concentrated purée)
60 ml (2 fl oz/¼ cup) pomegranate molasses, plus extra for drizzling
50 g (1¾ oz) feta cheese, crumbled
40 g (1½ oz/¼ cup) pine nuts

Preheat the oven to the highest temperature it will reach (not fan forced). Place a heavy-based baking tray or pizza stone on the middle shelf of the oven.

Divide the dough into 4 pieces. Using your hands or a rolling pin, roll out each piece on a lightly floured work surface into a 25 cm (10 inch) long oval. Spread a teaspoon or so of semolina on the pizza tray or a thin baking tray. Lay the rolled-out dough on top and make sure it can move around. Divide the lamb topping among the pizzas, leaving a 2 cm (¾ inch) border. Scatter with the feta and pine nuts, then slide the pizza onto the pizza stone or preheated baking tray and cook for 4–5 minutes until crisp on the bottom. You can cook up to 2 pizzas at a time depending on the size of your stone. Remove from the oven and drizzle with a little extra pomegranate molasses. Serve immediately.

GET AHEAD The dough can be made up to 2 days ahead and refrigerated. Use only ½ teaspoon of yeast if doing so and allow it to come to room temperature before making the pizzas. One day before, the topping can be prepared in full. Put the pizza together and cook it just before you want to serve.

The aromas of cinnamon and other spices permeate the streets in Morocco, from the market stalls to the footpaths. Tagines are made streetside in individual clay pots that bubble away for hours, making dreamy smells for passersby. Essaouira, a windy seaside town, is where I encountered this light stew. After eating a lot of lamb in Marrakesh it made a refreshing change.

CHERMOULA, TOMATO & FISH TAGINE

PREPARATION: 20 MINUTES, PLUS 30-60 MINUTES MARINATING • COOKING: 25 MINUTES • SERVES: 4-6

800 g (1 lb 12 oz) firm white fish fillets
  such as tilapia, swordfish, halibut
  or barramundi cod
150 g (5½ oz) small new potatoes
1 tablespoon olive oil
2 onions, thinly sliced
3 cm (1¼ inch) piece ginger, peeled,
  finely chopped
½ small piece preserved lemon, pith
  discarded, skin rinsed and chopped
1 tablespoon tomato paste
  (concentrated purée)
10 cherry tomatoes, halved
200 ml (7 fl oz) fish or vegetable
  stock

Steamed couscous, lemon wedges
  and chopped coriander (cilantro)
  leaves, to serve

Chermoula
1 large handful of coriander (cilantro)
  leaves and stalks
2 teaspoons ground hot paprika
2 teaspoons ground coriander
2 teaspoons ground cumin
juice of 2 lemons
2 tablespoons extra virgin
  olive oil
2 garlic cloves

To make the chermoula, process all the ingredients with a pinch of salt in a blender until smooth.

Cut the fish into large chunks and put it in a non-metallic dish, pour on half the chermoula and stand for 30-60 minutes.

Meanwhile, boil the potatoes in lightly salted water until tender. Drain and set aside.

To make the tagine base, heat the olive oil in a large saucepan over medium-high heat. Add the onion and ginger, season with salt and freshly ground black pepper and cook for 10 minutes or until soft. Add the remaining chermoula, preserved lemon, tomato paste, cherry tomatoes and stock. Bring to the boil, then reduce the heat to low and simmer for 10 minutes.

Add the fish and cooked potatoes to the saucepan containing the tagine base and cook for 5 minutes or until the fish is just cooked through. Serve the tagine, sprinkled with extra coriander, steamed couscous and lemon wedges.

GET AHEAD Make the chermoula and the base for the tagine earlier in the day, cover and refrigerate.

Cardamom and caramel make a formidable sauce for this pillow-soft cake studded with chopped dates. Scoop some ice cream or crème fraîche over it, sprinkle with the bashed brittle and indulge your friends after a Middle Eastern feast.

STICKY DATE CAKE WITH PISTACHIO BRITTLE & CARDAMOM TOFFEE SAUCE

PREPARATION: 15 MINUTES, PLUS 10 MINUTES SOAKING • COOKING: 55 MINUTES • SERVES: 4–6

200 g (7 oz) pitted dates, preferably
   soft medjool dates, finely chopped
80 ml (2½ fl oz/⅓ cup) boiling water
100 g (3½ oz) unsalted butter,
   softened
220 g (7 oz/1 cup) caster
   (superfine) sugar
2 eggs
175 g (6 oz) plain (all-purpose) flour
1½ teaspoons baking powder
60 ml (2 fl oz/¼ cup) milk

Ice cream, to serve

Pistachio brittle
75 g (2¾ oz) pistachio nut kernels,
   chopped
100 g (3½ oz) caster (superfine)
   sugar

Cardamom toffee sauce
200 g (7 oz) unsalted butter,
   chopped
250 ml (9 fl oz/1 cup) pure cream
   (35% fat)
350 g (12 oz) soft dark brown
   (muscovado) sugar
¼ teaspoon ground cardamom

Preheat the oven to 180°C (350°F) or 160°C (315°F) fan forced. Lightly grease a 20 cm (8 inch) square cake tin.

Put the dates in a bowl and pour the boiling water over them. Set aside for 10 minutes or until the water is absorbed.

Using an electric mixer fitted with the beater attachment, beat the butter and caster sugar until light and fluffy. Add the eggs, one at a time, beating well after each addition. Sift the flour and baking powder into the bowl, then stir in the milk and dates and continue stirring until well combined. Spoon the mixture into the prepared tin and bake for 40–50 minutes or until a skewer comes out clean. Remove from the oven and allow to stand while you prepare the sauce.

Meanwhile, to make the pistachio brittle, line a baking tray with baking paper and spread the nuts on the tray. Put the sugar in a heavy-based non-stick saucepan over medium heat. Don't stir, as it will cause the sugar to crystallise, simply tilt the pan when the sugar at the edge starts to go brown faster than the middle. When the sugar is evenly coloured to a light caramel, pour it over the nuts and stand for about 10 minutes to set. Break the brittle into pieces, making some quite fine and leaving others in larger pieces for serving.

To make the cardamom toffee sauce, put all of the ingredients in a heavy-based saucepan. Cook over low heat until the sugar dissolves, then increase the heat to medium and simmer rapidly for 5 minutes or until thick and dark. Serve the warm date cake and the hot toffee sauce with vanilla ice cream and a sprinkling of pistachio brittle

GET AHEAD The cake can be made earlier in the day, cooled and covered with foil. The toffee sauce can be prepared 2 days before, then covered and refrigerated. Reheat just before serving. Make the brittle up to 3 days ahead and store in an airtight container.

EXTRAS & SIMPLE SIDES

RICE VERMICELLI PILAFF

PREPARATION: 10 MINUTES • COOKING: 30 MINUTES • SERVES: 4–6 AS A SIDE

This buttery rice vermicelli pilaff is a tasty accompaniment to meat dishes such as the Spice-crusted Chicken with Pomegranate Salad (see page 108) and the Saffron Chicken & Cherry Tomato Kebabs (see page 117).

50 g (1¼ oz) dried vermicelli egg noodles
1 tablespoon olive oil
20 g (¾ oz) butter
2 onions, thinly sliced
250 g (9 oz/1¼ cups) basmati rice
600 ml (21 fl oz) vegetable or chicken stock

Put the noodles in a frying pan and dry-fry, shaking constantly, over low heat for 3–4 minutes until golden, then remove from the heat.

Heat the olive oil and the butter in a medium heavy-based saucepan over medium heat. Add the onion, season with salt and freshly ground black pepper and cook for 10 minutes or until golden. Add the rice and toasted noodles and stir for 1 minute, then add the stock. Cover the pan with a lid, reduce the heat to low and cook for 15 minutes until the rice is cooked. Remove the pan from the heat and use a fork to fluff the rice.

Variation: Saffron rice pilaff
Omit the vermicelli and add ½ teaspoon of saffron threads when you add the stock.

GRILLED FLATBREAD

PREPARATION: 20 MINUTES, PLUS 2 HOURS PROVING • COOKING: 15 MINUTES • MAKES: 6–8 FLATBREADS

Making your own flatbread at home is simple, especially if you have an electric mixer with a dough hook. No clay oven is required! It's the same as making pizza only easier. I griddle it, pan-fry it or throw it straight onto a hot barbecue.

1 teaspoon dried yeast
1 teaspoon sugar
350 ml (12 fl oz) warm water
500 g (1 lb 2 oz/3⅓ cups) plain (all-purpose) flour or strong flour, plus extra for kneading and rolling
1 teaspoon salt

Combine the yeast, sugar and water in a small bowl and stand for 5–10 minutes or until foamy. This is important because it means the yeast is working. If it doesn't foam, throw it out and start again.

Put the flour and salt in the bowl of an electric mixer fitted with the dough hook and mix on low speed. Add the yeast mixture and mix until the dough comes together into a ball. If the bottom is still sticking then add a couple of tablespoons of flour to allow it to come free. Knead in the electric mixer for 10 minutes or until smooth and elastic. (Alternatively, the dough may be hand-mixed in a bowl and kneaded on a floured work surface.)

Transfer to a lightly oiled bowl and turn to coat, then cover with plastic wrap and stand in a warm place for 2 hours or until doubled in size.

Divide the dough into 4 pieces. Using your hands, stretch each piece on a lightly floured surface into a 30 cm (12 inch) circle. Heat a large frying pan or chargrill pan over high heat until very hot. Dry fry or grill the flatbread for 1–2 minutes on each side until puffed and small grill marks appear. I also like to cook these on my barbecue using indirect heat. You don't need any oil, just a bit of flour on the surface, then close the lid and cook for 1–2 minutes on each side.

FATTOUSH

PREPARATION: 25 MINUTES • COOKING: 10 MINUTES • SERVES: 4–6

I never tire of making this chopped vegetable salad laced with crisp pita nuggets and bracing pomegranate dressing.

1 baby gem lettuce, roughly chopped
6 radishes, trimmed and thinly sliced
200 g (7 oz) cherry tomatoes, halved
3 Lebanese (short) cucumbers, cut into large dice
4 spring onions (scallions), thinly sliced
1 red capsicum (pepper), seeds and membranes discarded, cut into 2 cm (¾ inch) dice
small handful of chopped dill
small handful of flat-leaf (Italian) parsley
small handful of mint

Crispy pitta
2 pitta breads, cut into 2 cm (¾ inch) pieces
1 tablespoon extra virgin olive oil
3 teaspoons sumac, plus extra for serving

Dressing
1 small garlic clove, crushed with 1 teaspoon sea salt
2 tablespoons lemon juice
1 tablespoon red wine vinegar
1 tablespoon pomegranate molasses
45 ml (1½ fl oz) extra virgin olive oil

Preheat the oven to 200°C (400°F) or 180°C (350°F) fan forced.

To make the crispy pitta, spread out the bread pieces on a large oven tray. Drizzle with the olive oil and sprinkle with the sumac and lots of salt and freshly ground black pepper. Bake for 8 minutes or until golden. Remove from the oven and set aside.

To make the dressing, put all of the ingredients in a jar with a fitted lid and season with salt and pepper. Seal the jar and shake to combine well.

Place the salad ingredients in a large bowl. Just before serving, pour the dressing over, add the crisp pitta and gently toss.

SPINACH WITH ORANGE, FETA & WARM RAISIN DRESSING

PREPARATION: 15 MINUTES • COOKING: 10 MINUTES • SERVES: 4–6

If you want to stretch your meze or serve a fresh salad with meat and rice, look no further.

1 pitta bread, coarsely torn
100 g (3½ oz) raw almonds, coarsely chopped
1 tablespoon extra virgin olive oil
1 teaspoon Aleppo pepper or sumac
200 g (7 oz) baby spinach leaves
2 small seedless oranges, skin and pith removed, sliced thickly
50 g (1¾ oz) feta cheese, crumbled
½ small onion, thinly sliced

Dressing
60 ml (2 fl oz/¼ cup) extra virgin olive oil
1 garlic clove, thinly sliced
2 tablespoons sherry vinegar
1 tablespoon honey
2 tablespoons sultanas (golden raisins), soaked in boiling water for 5 minutes, drained

GET AHEAD The dressing can be made 2–3 hours before and left at room temperature. The almond pitta crumbs can be made earlier in the day, allowed to cool and stored in an airtight container. The salad is best made shortly before eating.

Preheat the oven to 200°C (400°F) or 180°C (350°F) fan forced.

Chop the pitta bread in a food processor until chunky breadcrumbs form. Spread them out on an oven tray with the almonds and drizzle with the olive oil. Season with salt and freshly ground black pepper, then sprinkle with the Aleppo pepper or sumac and bake for 5–6 minutes until golden. Remove from the oven and set aside.

Put the spinach in a large bowl or on a platter. Top with the orange slices, then scatter with the crumbled feta, sliced onion and toasted bread mixture.

To make the dressing, put the olive oil and garlic in a small frying pan over medium heat. Cook for 2 minutes or just until golden. Add the remaining ingredients and a pinch of salt and whisk together until well combined. Pour the warm dressing over the salad and toss gently. Serve immediately.

THE BEST OF CHINA & TAIWAN

HOT & SOUR

WITH SPECIAL SALT

Boiled Pork Dumplings with Tangy Dipping Sauce
(see page 138).

Jiaozi (pot sticker) dumplings (the kind with a pleated edge) can be fried, steamed, or—my favourite method—boiled. The wrapper goes velvety soft and keeps the pork and water chestnut filling juicy. You can buy wrappers from any Asian grocery, but once you bite into the fat chewy dough, I think you'll be sold on why home-made dough is worth it. This recipe makes 50 dumplings, which sounds like a lot, but since you've gone to the trouble you might as well eat half and freeze the rest for another occasion.

BOILED PORK DUMPLINGS WITH TANGY DIPPING SAUCE

PREPARATION: 1 HOUR, PLUS 1 HOUR STANDING • COOKING: 25 MINUTES • MAKES: 50 DUMPLINGS

300 g (10½ oz/2 cups) plain
 (all-purpose) flour
185 ml (6 fl oz/¾ cup)
 just-boiled water

Filling
3 cm (1¼ inch) piece ginger, peeled,
 roughly chopped
1 garlic clove
4 spring onions (scallions), chopped
10 tinned whole water chestnuts
300 g (10½ oz) minced (ground) pork
3 teaspoons shaoxing rice wine
3 teaspoons sesame oil
3 teaspoons soy sauce
2 teaspoons cornflour (cornstarch),
 plus extra for dusting

To make the dough, put the flour and a good pinch of salt in a food processor. With the motor running, add the just-boiled water and process until the dough comes together into a ball. If it is too soft, add another tablespoon of flour. (Alternatively, put the flour in a bowl and slowly pour in the hot water until the dough comes together.) Using lightly oiled hands, knead the dough for 2 minutes on a work surface, then shape into a ball and transfer to a lightly oiled bowl. Cover with plastic wrap and stand at room temperature for 1 hour.

Meanwhile, to make the filling, put the ginger, garlic and spring onion in a food processor and pulse until finely chopped. Add the water chestnuts and pulse until coarsely chopped. Add the remaining ingredients and pulse again until just combined. Remove and reserve in a bowl.

To make the dipping sauce, combine all of the ingredients in a small bowl and set aside.

Cut the dough into 4 pieces and place 3 pieces under a damp cloth while you roll out the first piece. Roll out the dough on a lightly cornflour-dusted work surface until it is just less than 3 mm (⅛ inch) thick. Using a 7.5 cm (3 inch) pastry cutter, cut out rounds from the dough and lay them on a cornflour-dusted tray. Cover with a tea towel (dish towel) and repeat with the remaining dough.

Dipping sauce
50 ml (1¾ fl oz) Chinese black vinegar
1 tablespoon finely grated ginger
1½ tablespoons roasted chilli oil
  (with the chilli sediment too),
  plus extra for drizzling
3 teaspoons caster (superfine) sugar
50 ml (1¾ fl oz) light soy sauce

Line a tray with baking paper and dust with cornflour. To make the dumplings, hold a round of dough in the palm of your hand. Place 1 teaspoon of the filling in the centre. Bring the sides of the dough up around it and pinch the middle together. Make little pleats on the front edge of the wrapper and then press it to the back edge. (You can also just press the edges together without pleats.) Bend the two edges around towards each other like a crescent. Place the dumpling on the cornflour-dusted tray and repeat with the remaining wrappers and filling.

Bring a large saucepan of water to the boil. Have 250 ml (9 fl oz/1 cup) cold water ready. Cooking in batches of 10, put the dumplings and the cold water in the saucepan and cook for 5 minutes or until the water returns to the boil and the dumplings float to the top.

Use a slotted spoon to scoop the dumplings out. Drain well, then place them on a big platter drizzled with a little chilli oil to keep them from sticking.

Serve the dumplings immediately with small bowls of dipping sauce and a big container of chopsticks so everyone can dig in.

GET AHEAD The uncooked dumplings can be refrigerated for up to 24 hours or frozen for up to 3 months. Store in a single layer between cornflour-dusted sheets of baking paper, covered with plastic wrap. After they are frozen, you can transfer them to a resealable plastic bag or airtight container. Boil them straight from the freezer for best results. Bring the water to a boil and instead of adding 250 ml (9 fl oz/1 cup) cold water add 500 ml (17 fl oz/2 cups) instead. You will get a wonderful result.

The special salt in these prawns is made up of the umami flavours of sichuan peppercorns and chillies which create a slightly numbing effect on the tongue. Sichuan peppercorns are not actually a peppercorn but a flower bud. When combined with chilli, they are a powerful flavouring for stir-fries or fried food.

SPECIAL SALT PRAWNS WITH CRISPY GARLIC, ONIONS & CHILLI

PREPARATION: 20 MINUTES • COOKING: 10 MINUTES • SERVES: 4–6

vegetable oil, for frying
2 garlic cloves, very thinly sliced
2 fresh long red chillies, cut into
 1 cm (⅜ inch) slices
24 large raw prawns, peeled
 and deveined

Iceberg lettuce leaves and chopped
 spring onions (scallions), to serve

Special salt
2 teaspoons sichuan peppercorns
4 black peppercorns
3 teaspoons sea salt flakes
large pinch of chilli flakes
30 g (1 oz/¼ cup) cornflour
 (cornstarch)

Chilli dipping sauce
1 garlic clove
1 large dried chilli, or sliced fresh chilli
2 teaspoons soft brown sugar
juice of 2 limes
2 teaspoons fish sauce

To make the special salt, toast the sichuan and black peppercorns in a small dry frying pan over medium heat for 1 minute or until fragrant. Allow to cool, then finely grind in a mortar and pestle or spice grinder. Pour into a bowl and stir in the salt, chilli flakes and cornflour.

To make the dipping sauce, crush the garlic and chilli in a mortar and pestle or finely chop together and transfer to a bowl. Add the remaining ingredients, then check the balance of flavours. It should taste sweet, salty and spicy: adjust if necessary.

Heat 7.5 cm (3 inches) of vegetable oil in a large wok or large heavy-based saucepan. When a piece of bread dropped into the oil sizzles quickly, the oil is ready. Have a slotted spoon and a tray lined with paper towel ready by the wok. Add the garlic and chilli and stir for 20 seconds or until light golden. Remove with the slotted spoon and drain on one end of the paper towel. Toss the prawns in the special salt, shake off the excess and deep-fry, in batches, for 1–2 minutes or until crisp at the edges and starting to curl. Remove with a slotted spoon and drain on the paper towel.

Serve the fried prawns in lettuce leaves, scattered with the fried garlic and chilli, with the chopped spring onion in a bowl of the dipping sauce.

GET AHEAD The special salt mix and the dipping sauce can be made earlier in the day and stored in separate airtight containers. Clean the prawns and store them in the refrigerator wrapped in baking paper (plastic makes them sweat). Fry just before serving.

Bao Buns with Spicy Chicken
(see page 144).

Bao, or baozi, are steamed buns filled with chopped meat (usually char siu barbecued pork) that are a prized regular in the yum cha (dim sum) carts. They are wildly popular right now with food trucks and probably set to become the next worldwide food craze. There is something about the cushy lighter-than-air bun and spicy sauce in the centre that makes people go weak at the knees. The dried milk powder gives the buns a sweet taste but if you don't have it, they still work really well.

BAO BUNS WITH SPICY CHICKEN
PREPARATION: 30 MINUTES, PLUS 1–2 HOURS PROVING • COOKING: 25 MINUTES • MAKES: 16 BUNS

350 g (12 oz/2⅓ cups) plain (all-purpose) flour

1½ tablespoons caster (superfine) sugar

3 teaspoons dried milk powder (optional)

2 teaspoons baking powder

1½ teaspoons fast-action or instant yeast

200 ml (7 fl oz) warm water

1½ tablespoons vegetable oil

Roasted chilli sauce, to serve

To make the dough, put the dry ingredients and a pinch of salt in the bowl of an electric mixer fitted with the dough hook. Mix on low speed until well combined. Add the water and vegetable oil and knead in the mixer for 8–10 minutes or until smooth and soft. Alternatively, to make by hand, put the dry ingredients in a mound on a work surface and make a well in the centre. Mix the yeast with the water and oil, then pour into the well and start mixing until the dough comes together. Knead by hand for 8–10 minutes or until smooth and soft.

Transfer the dough to a lightly oiled bowl, cover with plastic wrap and stand in a warm place for 1–2 hours until doubled in size.

Meanwhile, to make the filling, cut the chicken into 3 cm (1¼ inch) pieces. Heat the sesame oil in a large frying pan over medium–high heat and cook the chicken until golden. Add the spring onion and cook for 1 minute, then add all of the remaining ingredients and simmer for 5 minutes or until the sauce has thickened. Pour into a bowl, stand until slightly cooled, then refrigerate until completely cold.

When the dough has doubled in size, punch it down to expel the gas and knead for another minute. Divide the dough in half and roll out each piece into a fat cylinder. Cut each cylinder into 8 pieces. Roll out all of the pieces on a very lightly floured work surface into 7.5 cm (3 inch) rounds. You don't need much flour because the dough is quite elastic. Hold a disc in the palm of your hand and put 2 teaspoons of the cold filling in the centre. Bring the sides of the disc up and pinch them together at the top like a flower bud. Place each bun, seam side down, on a small square of baking paper.

Filling

500 g (1 lb 2 oz) boneless, skinless chicken thighs

3 teaspoons sesame oil

2 spring onions (scallions), chopped

2 tablespoons hoisin sauce

3 teaspoons soy sauce

1½ tablespoons honey

½ teaspoon Chinese five spice

½ teaspoon chilli flakes

1 teaspoon cornflour (cornstarch), dissolved in 3 teaspoons shaoxing rice wine

Cooking in batches if necessary, put the buns in a large bamboo or metal stacked steamer basket, making sure they don't touch each other. Make sure the steamer basket fits snugly over the saucepan or wok, then fill the bottom of the saucepan or wok with water and bring it to the boil. Set the steamer over the boiling water and cook for 10–12 minutes until the buns are cooked through. Serve immediately with roasted chilli sauce.

Variation: Bao filled with pork belly, cucumbers and sriracha

These are 'hamburger' type buns made with the same dough but folded over instead of wrapped around the filling. Make the dough recipe as above, then roll each piece out into an ellipse about 13 cm (5 inches) long. Fold in half and place on a small square of baking paper. Steam for 5 minutes or until cooked through. Split open the buns and fill with sliced crisp pork belly (see recipe for Basque Pork Belly Pintxos on page 84, but rub the meat with 2 teaspoons Chinese five spice instead of the cumin, fennel and paprika). Squirt in some sriracha, add slices of cucumber and some spring onion for an amazing sandwich.

GET AHEAD You can assemble the buns and freeze them in a single layer on a tray lined with baking paper, covered with plastic wrap. After they are frozen, transfer to a resealable plastic bag or airtight container. Steam straight from the freezer for best results.

Better known as kung pao, this blistering Sichuan stir-fry is a takeaway classic just about anywhere. Black vinegar and dark soy sauce zip up the sauce and the salty peanuts give it crunch. I've kept the dried chillies pretty middle ground. Not all of us want to sweat through our dinner so adjust them depending on your heat tolerance. The chillies are solely there to infuse flavour: be sure to leave them in large pieces so no one accidently eats one!

GUNPOWDER CHICKEN WITH DRIED CHILLIES & PEANUTS

PREPARATION: 20 MINUTES, PLUS 1 HOUR MARINATING • COOKING: 15 MINUTES • SERVES: 4–6

8 boneless, skinless chicken thighs, quartered
1 tablespoon soy sauce
1 tablespoon shaoxing rice wine
2 tablespoons vegetable oil
10 dried long red chillies, stems and seeds removed
1 bunch spring onions (scallions), cut into 2.5 cm (1 inch) pieces
40 g (1½ oz/¼ cup) whole roasted peanuts
1 heaped teaspoon sichuan peppercorns, ground

Sauce
60 ml (2 fl oz/¼ cup) soy sauce
60 ml (2 fl oz/¼ cup) Chinese black vinegar or red rice vinegar
60 ml (2 fl oz/¼ cup) chicken stock
1 tablespoon shaoxing rice wine or dry sherry
2 teaspoons caster (superfine) sugar
2 teaspoons cornflour (cornstarch), mixed with 1 tablespoon water

Steamed rice, to serve

Combine the chicken, soy sauce and shaoxing rice wine in a bowl, cover and refrigerate for 1 hour.

Meanwhile, to make the sauce, combine all of the ingredients in a small bowl and set aside.

Heat half the vegetable oil in a large wok over high heat. Cook the chicken, in batches, until golden all over, then set aside. Add the remaining oil and cook the chillies for 1 minute, shaking the wok constantly. Return the chicken to the wok, add the spring onion, peanuts and ground sichuan pepper and stir-fry for 1 minute. Add the sauce and cook for another 1–2 minutes or until reduced and thickened. Serve immediately with steamed rice.

GET AHEAD On the morning of serving you can marinate the chicken, make the sauce, prepare the remaining ingredients and refrigerate everything until ready to stir-fry just before serving.

Based on the classic 'red-cooked pork', this version is just a little more special. Chinese black vinegar breaks up the richness and isn't as sour as other vinegars: it's more of a malted, sweet taste. It's perfect for slow-braising pork belly. Although it seems like a large amount of meat, it shrinks quite a bit while cooking. Eat it with steamed rice and pickled red chillies and take your pork love to new heights.

BLACK VINEGAR BRAISED PORK BELLY WITH PICKLED CHILLIES

PREPARATION: 25 MINUTES, PLUS 1 HOUR MARINATING • COOKING: 2 HOURS 10 MINUTES • SERVES: 6

1.3 kg (3 lb) skinless boneless
   pork belly
2 tablespoons soy sauce
200 ml (7 fl oz) shaoxing rice wine
   or dry sherry
1½ tablespoons vegetable oil
2 garlic cloves, thinly sliced
5 cm (2 inch) piece ginger, peeled
   and julienned
pinch of chilli flakes
100 ml (3½ fl oz) Chinese black vinegar
150 g (5½ oz/⅔ cup firmly packed)
   soft brown sugar
700 ml (24 fl oz) vegetable stock

Toasted sesame seeds, julienned
   spring onions (scallions), Smacked
   Cucumber Pickles (see page 160)
   and steamed rice, to serve

Pickled chillies
2 long red or bird's eye chillies, sliced
50 ml (1¾ fl oz) rice wine vinegar

CHINESE BLACK VINEGAR

Also known as chinkiang vinegar, it is used frequently in the Sichuan and Southern regions. Its smoky flavour adds a delicious sour depth to braises and dipping sauces. It is sold in some supermarkets and most Asian grocery stores. If you can't get it, substitute balsamic vinegar.

Cut the pork into 5 cm (2 inch) pieces and put it in a bowl. Add 1 tablespoon each of the soy sauce and shaoxing rice wine, toss to combine, then cover and refrigerate for 1 hour or overnight if time permits.

Heat half of the vegetable oil in a heavy-based saucepan over high heat. Cook the pork, in batches until brown on both sides, then remove from the pan and set aside. Add the remaining oil and cook the garlic, ginger and chilli flakes for 1–2 minutes or until golden. Add the vinegar, sugar, stock and the remaining soy sauce and rice wine and bring to the boil. Return the pork to the pan, reduce the heat to low, then cover and simmer for 1½–2 hours until the meat is tender. During the final half hour, remove the lid to allow the liquid to reduce.

Meanwhile, to make the pickled chillies, put the sliced chilli and rice wine vinegar in a small bowl and stand for 1 hour.

Serve the pork scattered with toasted sesame seeds and spring onion, accompanied by steamed rice and Smacked Cucumber Pickles.

GET AHEAD The entire dish and the pickled chillies can be made 2 days ahead, covered and refrigerated. Reheat in a covered saucepan over low heat until warm.

FAST OR SLOW COOKING You can cook this quickly in a pressure cooker in 30 minutes. Make it in two batches, as you should never fill the pot more than half full. You can also cook it on the 4-hour setting in a slow cooker.

The countryside in southern China is ridiculously gorgeous. Bright green rice paddies surround the old mountains and we could ride bicycles everywhere. A local woman made us this simple dish at her home: the tasty vegetarian offering was a welcome respite after many stir-fries that included all the bones and bits. Soaking the aubergines in water before cooking keeps them plump and juicy.

HOT & SOUR EGGPLANT

PREPARATION: 10 MINUTES, PLUS 30 MINUTES SOAKING • COOKING: 10 MINUTES • SERVES: 4–6 AS A SIDE

1 large eggplant (aubergine),
  cut into 4 cm (1½ inch) chunks
60 ml (2 fl oz/¼ cup) peanut
  (groundnut) oil
1 large onion, halved and thickly
  sliced into half moons
1 thumb-size fresh red chilli, halved,
  seeded, thinly sliced

Sauce
1 tablespoon light soy sauce
1 tablespoon soy sauce
2 tablespoons Chinese black vinegar
2 tablespoons caster (superfine)
  sugar
1 teaspoon cornflour (cornstarch),
  mixed with 1 tablespoon water

Place the chopped eggplant in a bowl of lightly salted water and stand for 30 minutes. Drain and pat dry well on a clean tea towel (dish towel).

To make the sauce, combine all of the ingredients in a small bowl and set aside.

Heat the oil in a large frying pan or wok over medium–high heat. When hot, cook the eggplant until browned on all sides. Keep the heat medium–high so they brown nicely; don't turn them too early but let them get a nice colour first. When browned, add the onion and chilli and cook for another 3–4 minutes or until the eggplant is soft.

Add the sauce, cover with a lid and simmer for 1–2 minutes until the sauce has slightly thickened and all the flavours have melded together.

GET AHEAD Chop and soak the eggplant earlier in the day, then cover and refrigerate (you can keep it all day in the water and drain it just before frying). Mix the sauce and chop the vegetables, cover and refrigerate. The dish can be made in full 1 hour before serving, covered and kept at room temperature. Gently reheat just before serving.

I won't lie: when I have a hangover I crave this chilli-laden pork dish from my local Chinese takeaway. Despite years of trying to coax the recipe out of the very shouty waitress, I haven't really gotten a bean out of her as to what's in it. Most likely a truckload of MSG and triple frying. I took my best shot at deciphering the components and came up with this stir-fried rendition. No deep-frying and no tummy ache later.

SPICY SALT & PEPPER PORK STIR-FRY
PREPARATION: 20 MINUTES • COOKING: 5 MINUTES • SERVES: 4

600 g (1 lb 5 oz) pork fillet, sinew removed
1 teaspoon sichuan peppercorns
1 teaspoon fennel seeds
1 teaspoon cumin seeds
1 teaspoon chilli flakes
large pinch of sea salt flakes
1½ tablespoons cornflour (cornstarch)
50 ml (1¾ fl oz) vegetable or peanut (groundnut) oil
1 thumb-size fresh red chilli, thinly sliced
3 garlic cloves, chopped
3 cm (1¼ inch) piece ginger, peeled and finely chopped
1 large onion, cut into thick half moons
50 ml (1¾ fl oz) soy sauce
50 ml (1¾ fl oz) shaoxing rice wine (or sherry)
3 teaspoons roasted chilli oil

ROASTED CHILLI OIL

There are many brands of roasted chilli oil in Asian grocery stores. Some are made solely of roasted chilli flakes and oil, while others—such as LaoGanMa—contain salted black beans and garlic and more chillies than oil. This is the condiment you'll see on the table in Asian restaurants. Be warned: the LaoGanMa roasted chilli oil is highly addictive and is good on just about everything. Noodles, stir-fries and curries are all buoyed by the murky but delicious sediment from the bottom of the jar.

Thinly slice the pork against the grain and put it in a shallow dish. Place the sichuan peppercorns, fennel and cumin seeds in a small frying pan over medium heat and dry-fry for 1 minute or until fragrant. Cool slightly, then finely grind in a mortar and pestle or spice grinder. Add the chilli flakes and sea salt, then sprinkle the spice mixture on both sides of the pork. Dust the pork with the cornflour on both sides.

Heat 2 teaspoons of vegetable oil in a large frying pan or wok over medium heat. Add the chilli, garlic and ginger and cook for 2 minutes until golden and crisp. Remove with a slotted spoon and drain on paper towel. Add a little more oil to the pan and cook the pork in small batches for 1 minute or until browned on both sides, adding a little extra oil for each batch. Set the pork aside, then add the remaining oil to the pan. Add the onion and cook over high heat for 2–3 minutes or until just soft. Return the pork to the pan with the chilli and garlic mixture, soy sauce, shaoxing rice wine and chilli paste and toss until heated through. Serve with steamed rice on the side.

GET AHEAD Toast and grind the spices and slice the meat earlier in the day. Cover and refrigerate until close to serving. You can also chop and sauté the chilli and garlic mixture and set aside. Just before serving, coat the meat in the cornflour mixture, pan-fry and then carry on with the remaining steps in the recipe.

This page and opposite: Five-spice Duck Legs with Pancakes (see page 154).

Forget buying little kits from the supermarket to make duck pancakes, you can easily make your own. Originally I had planned to do a recipe for a whole duck, slow roasted. But duck legs are faster, less messy and have lush stringy flesh. You can buy the pancakes in Asian grocery stores, frozen, or just use small flour tortillas if you can't get them.

FIVE-SPICE DUCK LEGS WITH PANCAKES

PREPARATION: 15 MINUTES • COOKING: 1 HOUR • SERVES: 4–6

6 duck Marylands (leg quarters)
2 star anise, ground
3 teaspoons Chinese five spice
1½ tablespoons soy sauce

Accompaniments
warm Chinese pancakes or small
    flour tortillas
plum or hoisin sauce
2 Lebanese (short) cucumbers,
    cut into batons
6 spring onions (scallions), julienned

Preheat the oven to 200°C (400°F) or 180°C (350°F) fan forced.

Rub the duck skin with the combined ground spices, then brush the fleshy side with the soy sauce. Place the duck in a baking dish, skin-side up, cover with foil and roast for 45 minutes. Remove the foil, then increase the oven temperature to 220°C (425°F) or 200°C (400°F) fan forced and roast for another 15 minutes or until the meat pulls back from the bone and the skin is crisp. Remove from the oven and stand until cool enough to handle.

Shred the duck flesh and skin and serve on a platter with the pancakes, sauce, cucumbers and spring onion to roll up.

GET AHEAD The duck can be cooked the day before for 45 minutes. Cool, cover and refrigerate, then cook for the remaining 15 minutes on the day. The cucumbers can be cut into batons, covered and refrigerated earlier in the day. The spring onion can be julienned, wrapped in wet paper towel and refrigerated.

This recipe for poached chicken was packed in many suitcases when it left the Chinese island of Hainan. Since then it has made its way to Malaysia, Singapore, Vietnam, the Philippines and Thailand. It's one of the most popular street foods in the world and it's not fried. The whole bird is only simmered for 10 minutes and then for the rest of the cooking time it is left in the hot water with the lid on, keeping the flesh pillow-soft and full of juices. The stock is then used to make garlic rice and it is served up with a ginger chilli sauce. Chicken and rice is the ultimate comfort food and this is indeed one of the best preparations.

HAINANESE POACHED CHICKEN

PREPARATION: 15 MINUTES, PLUS 1 HOUR STANDING • COOKING: 20 MINUTES • SERVES: 4

1.2 kg (2 lb 10 oz) whole chicken, preferably corn-fed, free-range
2 teaspoons vegetable oil
2 garlic cloves, finely chopped
200 g (7 oz/1 cup) basmati or other long-grain rice
2 Lebanese (short) cucumbers, shaved into ribbons with a vegetable peeler
1 small handful of coriander (cilantro) leaves, coarsely chopped

Sweet soy and chilli dipping sauce
2 thumb-size red chillies, seeded, finely chopped
3 cm (1¼ inch) piece ginger, peeled and finely chopped
1 garlic clove, finely chopped
50 ml (1¾ fl oz) kecap manis (sweet soy sauce)
3 teaspoons rice vinegar
1½ tablespoons caster (superfine) sugar

Put 4 litres (140 fl oz/16 cups) of water in a large stockpot or saucepan and bring to the boil over high heat. Add the whole chicken and simmer for 10 minutes. Turn off the heat, cover with a lid and stand for 1 hour without removing the lid. It's important you use the right size chicken for this. If it is bigger than 1.2 kg then increase the cooking time from 10 minutes to 15 minutes.

Meanwhile, to make the dipping sauce, combine all of the ingredients in a small bowl. Alternatively, you could pulse it in a food processor instead of chopping by hand. Set aside.

About 10 minutes before the chicken is done, heat the oil in a saucepan over medium heat and cook the garlic for 30 seconds or until golden. Add the rice and stir for 1 minute or until well coated in the oil. Add enough of the stock from the pan with the chicken to cover the rice by 1 cm (⅜ inch). Cover and simmer for 10 minutes or until tender. Remove from the heat and leave covered while you cut the chicken.

Remove the chicken from the pan and discard any loose skin. Using kitchen scissors or a cleaver, cut the meat into large pieces. Arrange on a platter with the cucumber ribbons and coriander. Serve with the rice and dipping sauce.

GET AHEAD The dipping sauce can be made earlier in the day, then covered and refrigerated.

Chow fun is like the rice noodle version of pappardelle. You can buy them fresh or dried from Asian grocery stores. If you want to add spice, chop up a red chilli to stir-fry with the garlic.

BEEF CHOW FUN
PREPARATION: 15 MINUTES, PLUS 45 MINUTES CHILLING • COOKING: 10 MINUTES • SERVES: 4

500 g (1 lb 2 oz) piece beef skirt
(onglet), flank or bavette
1 teaspoon bicarbonate of soda
(baking soda)
1 teaspoon cornflour (cornstarch)
3 teaspoons soy sauce
400 g (14 oz) wide fresh rice noodles
or 250 g (9 oz) dried rice noodles
2 tablespoons sesame oil
2 garlic cloves, finely chopped
3 teaspoons minced ginger
250 g (9 oz) Asian greens such as
Chinese broccoli (gai larn) or choy
sum, cut into 2.5 cm (1 inch) pieces
2 large handfuls of fresh bean sprouts

4 spring onions (scallions), thinly
sliced, to serve

Sauce
2 tablespoons light soy sauce
2 tablespoons kecap manis
(sweet soy sauce)
1 tablespoon black bean sauce
2 tablespoons oyster sauce
2 tablespoons shaoxing rice wine

Wrap the beef tightly in plastic wrap and freeze for 30 minutes. This makes it easier to thinly slice the meat. Thinly slice the beef against the grain and place in a bowl. Add the bicarbonate of soda, cornflour and soy sauce, then season with freshly ground black pepper. Combine well and set aside for 15 minutes.

Meanwhile, to make the sauce, combine all of the ingredients in a bowl and set aside.

If using fresh noodles, rinse in warm water to break up, then cut in half lengthways. If using dried noodles, put them in a bowl and cover with warm water. Stand for 10 minutes, then drain. They will still be firm but will cook through in the pan.

Heat 2 teaspoons of the sesame oil in a large wok or frying pan over high heat. Cook half the beef for 1–2 minutes until nicely browned. Remove from the pan and repeat with another 2 teaspoons of oil and the remaining beef, then wipe the pan clean.

Add the remaining oil, and the garlic and ginger and cook over medium heat for 1 minute or until golden. Add the chopped Asian greens and stir-fry for 1 minute. Return the beef to the pan, add the noodles, sauce and bean sprouts and toss for 2 minutes or until heated through. Serve with the spring onion on the side to scatter over.

GET AHEAD Make the sauce and brown off the meat earlier in the day. Cover and refrigerate until just before serving. Prepare all the vegetables for the stir-fry.

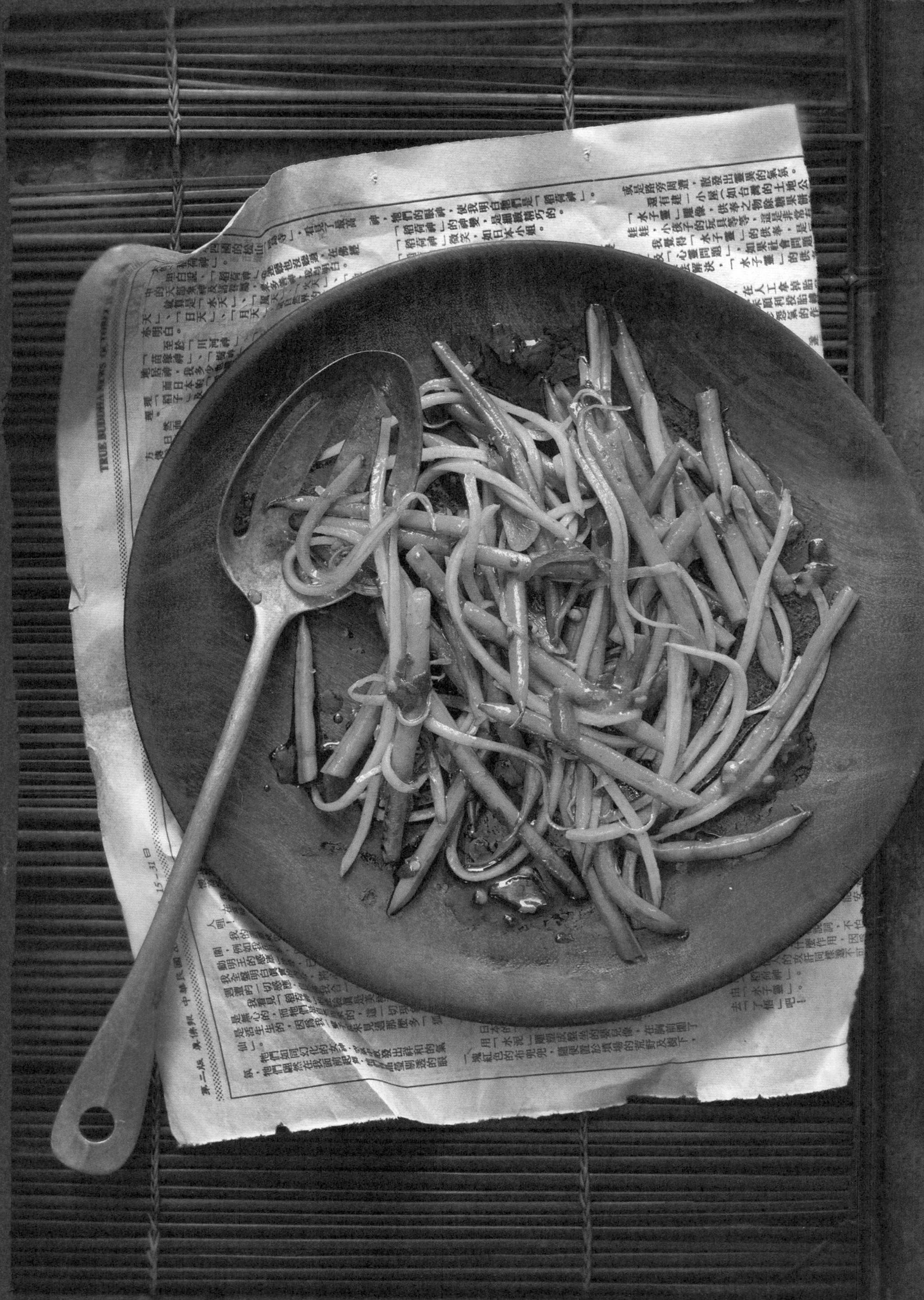

This is one of my stalwart Chinese side dishes and is a snap to throw together using crisp fresh vegetables. The ginger, spring onions and chilli paste give it a decided zing.

DRY-FRIED GREEN BEANS

PREPARATION: 10 MINUTES • COOKING: 10 MINUTES • SERVES: 4–6

1½ tablespoons peanut (groundnut) oil

300 g (10½ oz) baby green beans
or snake beans, cut into 4 cm
(1½ inch) pieces

1 large carrot, peeled and julienned

2 garlic cloves, finely chopped

2 cm (¾ inch) piece ginger, peeled,
finely chopped

3 spring onions (scallions),
finely chopped

1 tablespoon sambal oelek
(chilli paste)

1 tablespoon soy sauce

1 teaspoon sugar

Heat half the peanut oil in a wok over high heat. When hot, add the beans and carrot and stir-fry for 5 minutes or until they start to brown at the edges.

Add the remaining oil, then the garlic, ginger and spring onion and cook for 30 seconds or until golden. Add the sambal oelek, soy sauce and sugar and stir for another 30 seconds. Serve immediately.

GET AHEAD Chop all of the ingredients and keep covered and refrigerated until close to cooking and serving.

EXTRAS & SIMPLE SIDES

SMACKED CUCUMBER PICKLES
PREPARATION: 10 MINUTES • SERVES: 4–6

These tangy instant pickles take just minutes to make, and will compliment many spicy dishes.

1 telegraph (long) cucumber or 3 Lebanese (short)
  cucumbers, ends trimmed
3 teaspoons finely chopped garlic
1½ tablespoons caster (superfine) sugar
3 teaspoons light soy sauce
1½ tablespoons Chinese black vinegar
  or rice wine vinegar
1½ tablespoons chilli oil
1 teaspoon salt

Using a rolling pin or the flat side of a cleaver blade, smack the cucumbers so they split. Chop them into 2.5 cm (1 inch) pieces and put them in a bowl with the remaining ingredients. Toss together well and serve alongside any of the dishes in this chapter.

GET AHEAD The pickles can be made 2 hours before serving, then covered and refrigerated.

FORTUNE COOKIES

PREPARATION: 15 MINUTES, PLUS 30 MINUTES CHILLING •
COOKING: 30 MINUTES • MAKES: 18

Pen some daring predictions for the secret notes
inside these crisp vanilla-scented cookies. Of
course you can buy them from Chinatown (not
as fresh or delicious) but the personal messages
wouldn't be the same.

75 g (2¾ oz/½ cup) plain (all-purpose) flour, sifted
150 g (5½ oz/⅔ cup) caster (superfine) sugar
1 teaspoon natural vanilla extract
75 g (2¾ oz) unsalted butter, melted
18 small pieces of paper with chosen message
  scribed, then folded

Preheat the oven to 160°C (315°F) or 140°C (275°F)
fan forced. Line two large baking trays with baking
paper. Draw six 10 cm (4 inch) circles on the paper
on each tray.

    Put the flour, sugar, vanilla and butter in a bowl
and whisk until smooth. Cover and refrigerate for
30 minutes.

    Using the drawn circles as a guide, spoon one
scant tablespoon of batter into each 10 cm circle and
spread evenly with a palette knife. Only bake one tray
at a time, as you will need to work reasonably fast to
shape and fill the cookies before they harden. Bake
for 10 minutes or until light golden. Remove from
the oven and flip over with a palette knife. Working
quickly, place the message on one half of the cookie,
then fold in half, press to seal well and bring the
corners of the semicircle together.

    Set each cookie over the rim of a cake tin to
make the indent along the bottom. Repeat with
the remaining mixture.

GET AHEAD The cookies can be made 2 days in advance
and stored in an airtight container.

JAPAN & KOREA

MISO
HUNGRY

Spicy Tuna, Avocado & Rocket Sushi (see page 166).

If you love sushi making or Japanese cooking in general, you might want to think about investing in a small rice cooker. They cook the rice to perfection and, when making sushi, that's half the battle. If the rice is undercooked or overdone it takes down the final result. It's always wise to get a Japanese or Korean make as they are the smallest, least expensive and best quality. Rocket might sound like an inauthentic ingredient for sushi but its deep green colour and spicy bite sets off the creamy avocado and tuna.

SPICY TUNA, AVOCADO & ROCKET SUSHI

PREPARATION: 1 HOUR • COOKING: 15 MINUTES • MAKES: 8 ROLLS

200 g (7 oz) sashimi-grade tuna,
  sliced lengthways into 1.5 cm
  (⅝ inch) wide strips
2 teaspoons shichimi togarashi
  or mild chili powder (optional)
1 avocado, sliced into strips
50 g (1¾ oz) baby rocket (arugula)
  leaves
8 sheets nori

Pickled ginger and wasabi paste,
  to serve

Sushi rice
600 g (1 lb 5 oz) Japanese
  medium-grain rice
100 ml (3½ fl oz) rice wine vinegar,
  plus a little extra for rolling
1½ tablespoons caster (superfine)
  sugar

To make the sushi rice, put the rice in a bowl and cover it with cold water, then pour into a sieve and rinse. Repeat this process until the water runs clear. It is important to keep rinsing the rice to remove as much starch as possible. Drain well, then put the rice in a saucepan or rice cooker with 660 ml (22¾ fl oz) cold water. For the saucepan method, bring to the boil over medium–high heat, then reduce the heat to low, cover with a lid and simmer for 12 minutes or until the water is absorbed. Remove from the heat and stand, without removing the lid, for 10 minutes. If using a rice cooker, follow the manufacturer's instructions. Spread the warm rice over two trays.

Combine the rice wine vinegar, sugar and a large pinch of salt in a small bowl and stir until dissolved. Drizzle the mixture over the rice and gently work into the rice using two rubber spatulas until cool. Keep covered with tea towels (dish towels).

Sprinkle the tuna with the shichimi togarashi, if using. Using scissors, trim 5 cm (2 inches) off one long side of the nori sheets. This will keep the rolls slim. Have a bowl of water mixed with a little vinegar near your work area to use for dipping your hands into before picking up the rice. That way the rice won't stick and it keeps things fairly mess free.

Ponzu dipping sauce
60 ml (2 fl oz/¼ cup) soy sauce
1 tablespoon caster (superfine) sugar
2 tablespoons lemon juice

SHICHIMI TOGARASHI

A seven-spice blend that includes ground dried chilli, sichuan pepper, dried citrus peel, sesame seeds, poppyseeds, hemp seeds, ginger, garlic, shiso (perilla) and nori. Sprinkle it on any Japanese dish to add a spicy kick of umami.

Lay a sushi mat on a work surface with one long side facing you, then lay a sheet of nori, shiny-side down, on the mat. Dip your hands in the vinegar water. Pick up a large handful of rice and spread it over three-quarters of the nori, leaving a 4 cm (1½ inch) border at the top. Pat the rice down but don't make it too compact.

Make a shallow lengthways dent along the middle of the rice and place in it strips of tuna (end to end, trimming to fit), a couple of strips of avocado and a small handful of rocket. Bring the edge of the nori and rolling mat over the filling. Use your fingers to tuck it all in and then bring the front edge over to make a roll. Pull the mat back towards you so that it tightens everything. Moisten the edge of the wrapper with a little water and finish rolling it up. Place the roll, seam-side down, on a tray, cover loosely with plastic wrap and repeat with the remaining nori, rice and filling.

To make the ponzu dipping sauce, combine all of the ingredients in a small bowl and set aside.

Just before serving, using a large sharp knife cut each roll into 3 cm (1¼ inch) pieces, wiping the knife with a damp cloth after each slice. Serve with pickled ginger, wasabi paste and ponzu dipping sauce.

GET AHEAD You can make the sushi the night before. Store it on a tray lined with baking paper, cover with another sheet of baking paper, then cover in plastic wrap. Refrigerate for up to 24 hours and slice just before serving.

There are fast-food chains and trucks whose menus are solely devoted to this addictive chicken. Generally it's fried twice to crisp the skin and then rolled in a sweet vinegary chilli glaze made from the insanely good gochujang chilli paste. Since frying chicken on the bone can be a bit messy, I played around with the method to bake them crisp first. The end result is just as salivatingly good.

KOREAN FRIED CHICKEN WINGS WITH SPICY CHILLI GLAZE

PREPARATION: 15 MINUTES, PLUS OVERNIGHT BRINING • COOKING: 1 HOUR • SERVES: 4–6 AS A STARTER

1 kg (2 lb 4 oz) chicken wings, halved, tips removed

Brine
2 tablespoons caster (superfine) sugar
2 tablespoons rock or sea salt
3 garlic cloves, chopped
1 tablespoon soy sauce

Chilli glaze
60 g (2¼ oz/¼ cup) gochujang (Korean chilli paste)
4 tablespoons honey
2 tablespoons sake
4 tablespoons mirin (rice wine)
4 tablespoons rice vinegar
1 tablespoon black or white sesame seeds, toasted

GOCHUJANG (KOREAN CHILLI PASTE)

A thick Korean fermented soybean paste that includes red chilli and ground rice. Its spicy but sour taste adds a unique dimension to glazes, soups, stews and marinades. Buy it in tubs from Asian grocery stores and keep refrigerated once opened. If you think sriracha is good, this might become your new favourite.

Put the chicken wings in a resealable plastic bag or large bowl. Add all of the brine ingredients, combine well, then seal or cover with plastic wrap and refrigerate overnight.

Preheat the oven to 220°C (425°F) or 200°C (400°F) fan forced.

Drain, rinse and pat dry the chicken wings using paper towel. Place in a single layer in a large roasting tin and bake for 45 minutes, tossing several times during cooking.

Meanwhile, to make the glaze, combine all of the ingredients in a small bowl.

After the wings have roasted, drain off the excess oil and pour the glaze over the top. Bake for another 10–15 minutes until golden and sticky. Serve on a big platter.

GET AHEAD Marinate the chicken and make the glaze the day before, then cover and refrigerate. The next morning, roast the chicken for 35 minutes then remove it from the oven, cool and refrigerate. Just before serving, heat them again in the oven for 10 minutes, add the glaze and cook for another 10 minutes.

I admit it: I'm a bit of a dumpling junkie. Crisp, boiled or steamed, I cannot resist them. Gyoza are similar to jiaozi (pot stickers) as the bottom goes crispy while steaming. It's that extra crunch that gives it the glory. They are not hard to make; the trick is to pull the lid off just before all the liquid is gone and then let them move around the pan to crisp again. Feel free to substitute the same quantity of ground pork or chicken thigh meat for the prawns.

PRAWN & SAVOY CABBAGE GYOZA WITH PONZU DIPPING SAUCE

PREPARATION: 1 HOUR • COOKING: 5 MINUTES • MAKES: 40

40 gyoza wrappers (white round wrappers)
1½ tablespoons sesame oil, for frying

Filling
200 g (7 oz) savoy cabbage (winter cabbage), finely chopped
1 teaspoon salt
2 cm (¾ inch) piece ginger, peeled
4 spring onions (scallions), chopped
300 g (10½ oz) raw prawns, peeled
1½ tablespoons soy sauce
3 teaspoons sake
2 teaspoons sesame oil

Ponzu sauce
60 ml (2 fl oz/¼ cup) lemon juice
80 ml (2½ fl oz/⅓ cup) Japanese soy sauce
3 teaspoons sugar

To make the filling, put the cabbage and salt in a bowl and combine well. Stand for 15 minutes, then wrap the mixture in a clean tea towel (dish towel) and squeeze out as much liquid as possible.

Meanwhile, put the ginger and spring onions in a food processor and pulse until coarsely chopped. Add the prawns and pulse until finely chopped. Transfer to a bowl, add the cabbage, all of the remaining ingredients and a good grind of black pepper, then combine well. Refrigerate until ready to assemble the gyoza.

To make the ponzu sauce, combine all of the ingredients in a small bowl and set aside.

Hold a gyoza wrapper in the palm of your hand and spoon 3 teaspoons of filling in the middle. Lightly dampen the edges of the wrapper with a little water, then fold one half over and pinch the centre of the two rounded edges together to seal. Put the gyoza on a work surface and, working with the sides of the front wrapper, form 2–3 little pleats and press onto the back wrapper. This helps the dumpling sit flat and curves it slightly so they fit in the pan perfectly. Place the finished dumpling on a tray lined with baking paper and repeat with the remaining wrappers and filling.

CONTINUED

PRAWN & SAVOY CABBAGE GYOZA
WITH PONZU DIPPING SAUCE (CONTINUED)

Heat a large non-stick frying pan with a fitted lid over medium–high heat and pour 1½ teaspoons of sesame oil into the pan. Put 20 gyoza in the pan and cook for 1–2 minutes until golden. Add 60 ml (2 fl oz/¼ cup) water, cover and cook for 2 minutes. When most of the water has evaporated, remove the lid and shake the pan gently to make sure the dumplings aren't sticking. Drizzle another ½ teaspoon of sesame oil around the gyoza and cook for another couple of seconds until the bases are crisp.

Set the first batch aside to keep warm and repeat with the remaining gyoza, or freeze them for another meal. Serve gyoza hot with the ponzu dipping sauce.

GET AHEAD The night before you can make the dumplings and refrigerate them on a flour-dusted tray in between two sheets of baking paper and covered with plastic wrap. You can also freeze them and cook them straight from the freezer. Just add 100 ml (3½ fl oz) of water to the pan instead of 60 ml and cook them through. The ponzu can be made 2 days ahead, then covered and refrigerated.

NOTE It is very important to use frying pans with a decent non-stick surface. Older pans with worn surfaces or thin bottoms can cause sticking when cooking these dumplings.

The Japanese are noodle gurus, whether it be chewy buckwheat soba, egg ramen or delicate wheat somen; however, their triumph is the thick bouncy udon with its toothsome bite. I know making your own sounds very aspirational (or just insane) but it's no more effort than making home-made pasta. Fry them up yakisoba style (see method below) or make a comforting soup. A good broth is all you need, so either buy it or use my quick method below. Good Japanese grocery stores also sell quality frozen noodles, which is the next best thing to home-made.

HOME-MADE UDON NOODLES

PREPARATION: 30 MINUTES, PLUS 4 HOURS RESTING • COOKING: 3½ HOURS • SERVES: 4–6

1 tablespoon salt
225 ml (7¾ fl oz) warm water
450 g (1 lb 3 oz) plain (all-purpose) flour or 00 (pastry) flour, plus extra for rolling and dusting
2 large handfuls of chopped spring onions (scallions)
1 teaspoon shichimi togarashi (optional)

Chicken broth
4 chicken Marylands (leg quarters)
2 large carrots, peeled and quartered
4 celery stalks, quartered
2 onions, quartered
4 cm (1½ inch) piece ginger, halved
½ garlic bulb
2 tablespoons mirin (rice wine)
2 tablespoons light soy sauce

00 (PASTRY) FLOUR

Double zero (00) or doppio zero flour is a durum wheat flour. In the Italian wheat grading system, the numbers 2, 1, 0 and 00 indicate how much of the bran has been removed in the process of refining the flour. Double zero is the finest, prized for its silky texture and produces a delicate but chewy dough. It's predominantly used for pasta, pizza and pastry. 00 (pastry) flour is available in most supermarkets.

To make the broth, preheat the oven to 220°C (425°F) or 200°C (400°F) fan forced.

Put the chicken, carrot, celery and onion in a large roasting tin. Season and roast for 30 minutes or until golden. Remove from the tin and place everything including the fat and juices into a stockpot or large saucepan. Add the ginger and garlic and enough cold water to cover. Bring to the boil over high heat, then reduce the heat as low as possible. Skim any fat and impurities from the surface and place a lid on top, leaving it slightly askew. Simmer for 2–3 hours without stirring (stirring may make the broth cloudy), then remove from the heat and stand until cool. Skim the excess fat off the surface and strain the liquid into a clean saucepan, reserving the chicken and discarding the vegetables. Stir the mirin and soy sauce into the stock and season with salt and freshly ground black pepper. You should have about 1 litre (35 fl oz/4 cups) of stock.

Meanwhile, to make the noodles, dissolve the salt in the warm water. Put the flour in the bowl of an electric mixer fitted with the dough hook attachment. With the motor on low speed, add the water and knead for 8–10 minutes or until the dough is soft and smooth. Add 1 tablespoon of flour, if necessary, to help the dough come unstuck if it seems wet. Alternatively, put the flour in a mound on your work surface, make a well in the centre and then pour the salted water in. Gradually incorporate the flour until the dough comes together, then knead for 8–10 minutes. Transfer it to a bowl, cover tightly with plastic wrap and stand at room temperature for 3–4 hours to rest. To check if the dough is ready to use, make an indentation with your finger. If the dough bounces back, give it another hour, but if the dent remains the dough is ready to use.

CONTINUED

HOME-MADE UDON NOODLES (CONTINUED)

GET AHEAD You can make the broth up to 3 days before and keep refrigerated or frozen. You can also make the dough for the noodles and leave it covered in the refrigerator for 1 day. Bring it back to room temperature before rolling out. The noodles can be made up to 1 day in advance and stored in between sheets of baking paper, lightly dusted with cornflour, then covered with plastic wrap and refrigerated or frozen the same way. Boil the frozen noodles without defrosting.

Cut the dough into four pieces. Using a rolling pin, roll out each piece of dough on a lightly floured work surface into a 5 mm (¼ inch) thick rectangle. If the dough feels sticky, sprinkle both sides with a little extra flour. Use a sharp knife to cut into 5 mm (¼ inch) strips. Untangle the noodles and scatter them over a well-floured tray. You could also use a pasta maker on the thickest setting to roll each piece of dough and then cut into noodles using the fettuccine attachment.

To cook the noodles, bring a very large saucepan of water to the boil. Add the noodles slowly so they don't stick together. As soon as they are all in, add 250 ml (9 fl oz/1 cup) cold water, then bring it back to the boil. Add another cup of cold water and bring back to the boil again. By this stage the noodles should be al dente. If not, then repeat the process of adding water and returning to the boil until they are done. It should take about 6–8 minutes. Drain, rinse under cold running water until cold, then leave the noodles in a colander until using. Keep refreshing with cold water from time to time to keep them from sticking.

Bring the broth to a simmer. Meanwhile, remove and discard the chicken skin, then shred the meat. Divide the noodles, shredded chicken and spring onions among 4–6 serving bowls, then pour on the hot broth. Sprinkle with the shichimi togarashi, if using, and serve immediately.

Variation: Yaki udon
Combine 80 ml (2½ fl oz/⅓ cup) mirin (rice wine), 3 teaspoons Worcestershire sauce, 1½ tablespoons soy sauce and 3 teaspoons sugar in a bowl and set aside. Heat 1 tablespoon of sesame oil in a wok over high heat. Add 1 thickly sliced onion, 6 sliced shiitake mushrooms, ¼ thickly sliced white cabbage and 250 g (9 oz) thinly sliced pork fillet. Stir-fry for 5 minutes or until the pork is golden and crisp. Add 400 g (14 oz) of cooked udon noodles and toss until heated through. Add the sauce and toss for another minute or until well combined. Serves 2–4.

Izakaya, Japanese pubs or taverns, serve up unpretentious menus ranging from sashimi to yakitori or tempura. After office hours, these dark smoky joints are jammed with people downing cold beer while feasting on seriously good food. For very little money you can eat like a king in a buzzy bijoux setting. Small dishes are typical and this is one of my more memorable ones. If you want to make this more substantial then grill a steak or chicken breast to scoop up the sharp dressing.

TOMATO & AVOCADO SALAD WITH ONION SOY DRESSING & GARLIC CHIPS

PREPARATION: 10 MINUTES • COOKING: 5 MINUTES • SERVES: 6 • SEE PHOTOGRAPH ON PAGE 180

10 large radishes, trimmed, sliced
3 vine-ripened tomatoes, sliced
1 avocado, cut into chunky pieces
1 small bunch chives, snipped

Garlic chips
2 tablespoons vegetable oil
2 garlic cloves, thinly sliced
sea salt flakes

Onion soy dressing
1½ tablespoons soy sauce
juice of 1 lime
50 ml (1¾ fl oz) yuzu or grapefruit
   juice
1½ tablespoons caster (superfine)
   sugar
3 teaspoons finely grated ginger
2 red Asian shallots, finely chopped

To make the garlic chips, heat the oil in a small saucepan over medium heat. Cook the sliced garlic for about 1 minute until golden. Make sure the oil doesn't get too hot or the garlic will burn and become bitter. Remove the garlic chips with a slotted spoon and drain on paper towel. Sprinkle with sea salt.

To make the dressing, combine all the ingredients in a small bowl. Some soy sauce is saltier than others so taste and add more citrus or sugar if desired.

Arrange the radish and tomato slices with the avocado on a serving plate and pour the dressing over the salad. Scatter with the chives and garlic chips.

GET AHEAD The dressing and garlic chips can be made earlier in the day. Cover and refrigerate the dressing and keep the garlic chips in a sealed container. Chop the salad and add the dressing just before serving.

This is also known as bo ssäm, which translates as 'wrapped'. Traditionally it's made with slow roast pork shoulder or belly but it's also done with grilled steak or beef ribs (galbi). Now if you haven't heard of galbi, they are thinly sliced steaks cut through the 'dinosaur like' beef rib bones. In case you didn't get that, it's across the ribs instead of in between. You end up with mostly meat and a small bit of bone at the bottom. They don't need any slow cooking like the uncut ribs and are delicious with this bulgogi marinade. Most butchers will cut them for you, or you can just use rib eye steak instead.

KOREAN BEEF RIB BARBECUE
PREPARATION: 15 MINUTES, PLUS OVERNIGHT MARINATING • COOKING: 5 MINUTES • SERVES: 4

8 small rib eye steaks or galbi beef
   ribs, about 2 cm (¾ inch) thick
1 tablespoon sesame oil

Kimchi (see page 194) and Quick
   Japanese Cucumber Pickles
   (see page 193), to serve
16 large iceberg or butter lettuce
   leaves, to serve
200 g (7 oz) warm cooked Japanese
   medium-grain rice, to serve

Bulgogi marinade
60 ml (2 fl oz/¼ cup) soy sauce
75 g (2¾ oz/⅓ cup) caster (superfine)
   sugar
60 ml (2 fl oz/¼ cup) mirin (rice wine)
6 cm (2½ inch) piece ginger, peeled
6 garlic cloves, peeled
2 tablespoons chopped
   fresh pineapple
2 teaspoons chilli flakes or gochugaru
   (Korean chilli powder)
1½ tablespoons sesame oil

Chilli sauce
60 g (2¼ oz/¼ cup) gochujang
   (Korean chilli paste) or sriracha
1 tablespoon rice wine vinegar
2 tablespoons caster (superfine)
   sugar

To make the marinade, place all of the ingredients in a blender or food processor and process until finely chopped. Put the steak in a resealable plastic bag or a shallow dish and pour the marinade over the steaks. Seal or cover and refrigerate overnight.

To make the chilli sauce, combine all of the ingredients in a small bowl.

Heat a barbecue grill plate or a griller (broiler) to high heat. Remove the steaks from the marinade and pat dry. Drizzle with the sesame oil on both sides to keep from sticking. Cook for about 2 minutes on each side, then brush all over with some of the chilli sauce and cook for another 30 seconds on each side.

Serve with kimchi, cucumber pickle, lettuce and bowls of hot steamed rice. Traditionally, scissors are placed on the table to cut the beef into smaller pieces. Fill a lettuce leaf with some rice, pickles, beef and a drizzle of the chilli sauce.

GET AHEAD Marinate the beef and make the pickles the night before. Grill just before serving.

I wasn't awakened to the pleasures of tonkatsu before visiting Tokyo but it's now frequently part of my weekday supper repertoire. Coated in panko breadcrumbs and then shallow-fried until golden and crisp, it has a leg-up on your usual crumbed meat. The thick spicy sauce served alongside is like HP or steak sauce with soy and spicy mustard. Most Japanese buy the famous brand called 'Bulldog' but making your own is easy and you know exactly what's in it.

TONKATSU PORK WITH TANGY SLAW

PREPARATION: 30 MINUTES • COOKING: 15 MINUTES • SERVES: 4–6

700 g (1 lb 9 oz) pork tenderloin,
 fat trimmed
plain (all-purpose) flour, for dusting
3 eggs, lightly beaten
300 g (10½ oz/5 cups) panko
 breadcrumbs
vegetable or peanut (groundnut) oil,
 for shallow-frying

Lime wedges, to serve

Tangy slaw
1 small cabbage, about 400 g (14 oz),
 shredded
50 ml (1¾ fl oz) soy sauce
2 tablespoons yuzu juice or
 1 tablespoon each lime and
 grapefruit juice

Tonkatsu sauce
60 ml (2 fl oz/¼ cup) Worcestershire
 sauce
2 tablespoons soy sauce
2 tablespoons sugar
100 ml (3½ fl oz) tomato sauce
 (ketchup)
1 tablespoon sake
1 teaspoon English mustard

To make the slaw, put the shredded cabbage in a bowl of lightly salted water with some ice cubes and refrigerate for 30–60 minutes. This will help it stay crisp when you mix it with the dressing later. Drain the cabbage, spin dry in a salad spinner and transfer it to a bowl. Combine the soy sauce and yuzu juice in a small bowl and toss through the cabbage just before serving.

Meanwhile, to make the tonkatsu sauce, combine all of the ingredients in a small bowl and whisk until smooth.

Slice the pork tenderloin about 3 cm (1¼ inches) thick, cover with a piece of baking paper, then gently pound it with a rolling pin until it is 1.5–2 cm (⅝–¾ inch) thick. Put the flour, beaten egg and breadcrumbs in three separate shallow bowls. Season the pork with salt and pepper, then dust with flour, dip in the beaten egg and coat in breadcrumbs.

Heat 2 cm (¾ inch) of oil in a very large frying pan over medium–high heat. When hot, cook the pork in batches until brown and crisp on both sides. After 2 batches, you may want to wipe the pan clean and add clean oil. Cut the pork into 2.5 cm (1 inch) wide strips and serve it hot with the tangy slaw, tonkatsu sauce and lime wedges.

GET AHEAD The pork can be crumbed the night before, stored between sheets of baking paper on a tray, then covered with plastic wrap. The tonkatsu sauce can be made 2 days ahead, covered and refrigerated. Fry the pork cutlets just before serving as they are best crisp and hot.

This was another dish I devoured in one of Tokyo's many izakaya. Dark chicken meat is marinated, cut into pieces and deep-fried. Once again, I've amended this slightly, swapping the deep-frying for pan-frying. A cornflour dusting creates an uber golden crust and the final baking finishes it off. It's a simple dish and yet another way to make crispy chicken.

KARA'AGE CHICKEN WITH YUZU SOY DIPPING SAUCE & SPICY CHILLI MAYO

PREPARATION: 20 MINUTES, PLUS 1 HOUR MARINATING • COOKING: 15 MINUTES • SERVES: 4-6

8 boneless, skinless chicken thighs,
quartered
4 cm (1½ inch) piece ginger, peeled
and finely grated
2 garlic cloves, finely grated
2 tablespoons soy sauce
2 tablespoons mirin (rice wine)
125 g (4½ oz/1 cup) cornflour
(cornstarch) or rice flour, for dusting
vegetable oil, for pan-frying

Soy yuzu dipping sauce
2 tablespoons soy sauce
2 tablespoons yuzu juice or
1 tablespoon each lime and
grapefruit juice
1 tablespoon caster (superfine) sugar

Creamy spicy sauce
125 g (4½ oz) japanese Kewpie or
other mayonnaise
½ garlic clove, crushed
1 teaspoon lemon juice
1½ tablespoons sriracha or gochujang
(Korean chilli paste)

Put the chicken in a bowl with the ginger, garlic, soy sauce and mirin. Combine well, then cover and refrigerate for 1 hour or overnight if time permits: the longer the better.

Meanwhile, to make the sauces, combine the ingredients for each of the sauces in small serving bowls and set aside. Preheat the oven to 220°C (425°F) or 200°C (400°F) fan forced.

Drain the chicken and pat dry. Dust the chicken with the cornflour and shake off the excess. Heat two large frying pans over medium–high heat and pour 5 mm (¼ inch) of vegetable oil into each pan. When the oil is very hot, add the chicken pieces and cook without turning for 2–3 minutes until well browned. Turn and cook on the other side, then transfer the chicken to a baking tray and bake for 5 minutes. Serve the hot crisp chicken with the dipping sauces.

NOTE If you prefer home-made mayonnaise, use 125 g (4½ oz) of Lemon saffron aïoli (see page 76), leaving out the saffron, and add the sriracha or gochujang to make the Creamy spicy sauce.

GET AHEAD The chicken can be marinated and the sauces prepared the night before, then covered and refrigerated. Dust with the cornflour and fry just before serving.

Donburi are the rice bowl dishes of Japan. They are as comforting as a woolly blanket and lightning quick to prepare. Onions and chicken are poached in a soy and mirin liquid with egg mixed in and eaten over rice. Oyako translates to 'parent and child', which refers to the chicken and the egg.

OYAKODON CHICKEN & EGG RICE BOWL

PREPARATION: 15 MINUTES • COOKING: 25 MINUTES • SERVES: 4–6

100 ml (3½ fl oz) Japanese soy sauce

100 ml (3½ fl oz) mirin (rice wine)

100 ml (3½ fl oz) sake

200 ml (7 fl oz) dashi or vegetable stock

1½ tablespoons caster (superfine) sugar

2 large onions, sliced into half moons

700 g (1 lb 9 oz) boneless, skinless chicken thighs, cut into 3 cm (1¼ inch) pieces

2 eggs, lightly beaten

Steamed Japanese rice, pickled ginger, chopped spring onion and shichimi togarashi (optional), to serve

Combine the soy sauce, mirin, sake, stock and sugar in a saucepan over medium heat. Bring to the boil, then simmer for 2–3 minutes. Add the onion and simmer for 10 minutes or until soft. Add the chicken and simmer for another 10 minutes or until cooked through.

Just before serving, pour in the eggs and let them gently poach in the hot liquid. Serve with hot rice, pickled ginger, chopped spring onion and shichimi togarashi, if using.

GET AHEAD The entire dish up to the point of adding the egg can be made earlier in the day, then covered and refrigerated. Reheat in a saucepan and when it comes to a simmer, add the beaten egg.

It's a mouthful to pronounce but okonomi means 'as you like it'. This dish is sometimes called Japanese pancake or pizza. Numerous ingredients are added to the standard base of egg, cabbage and onion: seafood, pork, noodles or other vegetables. But you can make it as simple or as complex as you like. Sold at street markets or at restaurants with tabletop griddles, it's a soul-satisfying and inexpensive dish to prepare. After being seared and flipped, it gets a drizzling of mayonnaise and tonkatsu sauce and a scattering of pickled ginger and seaweed.

OKONOMIYAKI PANCAKES

PREPARATION: 15 MINUTES • COOKING: 10 MINUTES • SERVES: 2–4

250 g (9 oz/1⅔ cups) plain
  (all-purpose) flour
1 teaspoon baking powder
1 teaspoon salt
250 ml (9 fl oz/1 cup) cold dashi
  or vegetable stock
3 eggs
350 g (12 oz) green cabbage,
  coarsely chopped
1 potato or small sweet potato,
  peeled, grated, liquid squeezed out
3 spring onions (scallions), finely
  chopped, plus extra, to serve
1½ tablespoons chopped pickled
  ginger
60 ml (2 fl oz/¼ cup) sesame oil,
  for frying

Japanese Kewpie mayonnaise,
  Tonkatsu sauce (see page 178),
  shredded nori and pickled ginger,
  to serve

Put the flour, baking powder and salt into a large bowl. Add the stock and eggs and whisk until well combined. Add the cabbage, potato, spring onion and ginger and combine well.

Heat two frying pans over medium heat and pour a thin coating of sesame oil onto the bottom of each. Divide the pancake mixture between the pans and spread it across the pan. Cook for 5 minutes or until golden and crisp. Place a plate on top of the pan and hold on to it tightly as you invert the pancake onto the plate. Slide the pancake, cooked side up, back into the pan and cook the other side, adding a little more oil if necessary.

Serve hot with a dollop of mayonnaise and a drizzle of tonkatsu sauce, topped with a scattering of spring onions, shredded nori and pickled ginger.

GET AHEAD The vegetables can be chopped and grated 2 hours before. Keep the potato in cold water to prevent discolouring. Make the batter up to 1 hour before, but stir in the vegetables just before cooking.

The name sounds like some crazy board game but it's a Korean specialty of hot rice topped with seared vegetables, sometimes meat or chicken and a fried egg. A dollop of hot chilli paste is spooned over just before serving and it's all stirred together. It's the Korean equivalent of fried rice, but an amped-up spicy version. Traditionally it's served in a hot stone bowl called a dolsot, but a rice cooker can be just as good for serving up piping hot rice. It also forms a nice crust on the bottom similar to the stone bowl. I've made a veggie rendition, but if you want meat, use chopped chicken thighs or marinated thin slices of beef (use the Korean Beef Rib Barbecue recipe, page 177) and sear them up before preparing the other toppings. A julienne tool makes light work of cutting the vegetables.

BIBIMBAP

PREPARATION: 20 MINUTES • COOKING: 10 MINUTES • SERVES: 4–6

60 ml (2 fl oz/¼ cup) sesame oil
2 carrots, peeled and julienned
2 zucchini (courgettes), julienned
1 onion, halved and sliced into
    half moons
150 g (5½ oz) green beans, cut
    into 3 cm (1¼ inch) pieces
4–6 eggs
300 g (10½ oz) Japanese
    medium-grain rice, steamed
    (see Note)
2 tablespoons sesame seeds, toasted,
    to serve

Chilli sauce
60 g (2¼ oz/¼ cup) gochujang
    (Korean chilli paste) or use sriracha
60 ml (2 fl oz/¼ cup) rice wine
    vinegar
2 tablespoons caster (superfine)
    sugar

GET AHEAD The sauce can be made and the vegetables can be chopped earlier in the day, then covered and refrigerated. Make the rice and stir-fry just before serving.

To make the sauce, combine all of the ingredients in a small bowl and set aside.

It is important you have all your vegetables prepared and the rice steamed before you start cooking as it is a quick process. I like using a rice cooker because it cooks Japanese rice perfectly and keeps it toasty warm until you are ready.

Heat three frying pans or one wok and two frying pans over medium–high heat. Heat 1 tablespoon of the sesame oil in each pan until very hot. Cook the carrot and zucchini in one pan, the onion and beans in another and the eggs in the third. Keep them in their own pans so they don't get mixed up. Cook the veggies for 2–3 minutes, tossing a few times. Once they are done, remove from the heat. Cook the eggs, sunny side up, keeping the yolks runny. If you don't have room to fit all the pans on the stove at once, just cook them quickly in batches.

Serve bowls of hot rice, topped with the veggies in their own sections and a fried egg. Serve the chilli sauce separately: you pour a big spoonful of the chilli sauce on, sprinkle with toasted sesame seeds, and then toss everything together in your bowl.

NOTE If you don't have a rice cooker, here's how to prepare perfect Japanese rice: Put 300 g (10½ oz) Japanese medium-grain rice in a large bowl filled with cold water. Stir it with your hands, drain and repeat until the water is clear, about three times. Strain through a fine sieve. Pour the rice into a medium saucepan and cover with 375 ml (13 fl oz/1½ cups) water. Bring to the boil over medium heat, then reduce the heat to low, cover and simmer for 12–15 minutes or until the water is absorbed. Remove from the heat and leave covered for 10 minutes.

Yakitori: Tsukune Chicken Meatballs with
Teriyaki Sauce (see pages 188–89).

If you're wandering the streets of Tokyo in search of a yakitori street stall or izakaya, just follow your nose: the tantalising charcoal smoke will lure you in. The umami smell of the grill and the taro sauce will make you crazy with hunger. Most yakitori are very simple combinations: it's the charcoal grilling and the sauce that really makes it special. Choose the salmon, chicken meatballs or vegetables for a genius simple meal. You can use traditional teriyaki or try something a little different, like this mustard-spiked miso sauce. Skewer any of your favourite ingredients, then fire up the grill and brush with the sauces.

YAKITORI

PREPARATION: 20 MINUTES • COOKING: 10 MINUTES • SERVES: 6

60 ml (2 fl oz/¼ cup) light soy sauce
60 ml (2 fl oz/¼ cup) mirin (rice wine)
60 ml (2 fl oz/¼ cup) sake
juice of 1 lemon
40 g (1½ oz) caster (superfine) sugar

1 TERIYAKI SAUCE

PREPARATION: 10 MINUTES • SERVES: 4 (MAKES 250 ML/9 FL OZ/1 CUP)

Combine all of the ingredients in a small saucepan. Bring to the boil, then simmer over low heat for 5 minutes until thick and syrupy.

2 tablespoons sweet white miso
   (shiro miso)
2 tablespoons mirin (rice wine)
2 tablespoons yuzu juice or
   1 tablespoon each lime and
   grapefruit juice
1 tablespoon caster (superfine) sugar
1 teaspoon karashi (Japanese mustard)
   or ½ teaspoon hot English mustard

2 MISO SAUCE

(MAKES 145 ML/4¾ FL OZ)

Combine all of the ingredients in a small bowl and whisk until smooth.

300 g (10½ oz) skinless salmon fillet,
   pinbones removed, cut into 4 cm
   (1½ inch) cubes
2 spring onions (scallions), cut into
   4 cm (1½ inch) pieces
vegetable oil, for brushing
lightly toasted black or white sesame
   seeds and shichimi togarashi, for
   sprinkling

3 SALMON

(MAKES 12 SKEWERS)

Preheat a barbecue, chargrill pan or the grill (broiler) to high. If using wooden skewers, soak them in water for at least 10 minutes to prevent them from burning during cooking.

   Thread the salmon and spring onion pieces alternately onto the skewers and brush with oil on all sides. Cook for 2 minutes on each side. Brush with Miso Sauce or Teriyaki Sauce until thickly glazed, then sprinkle with sesame seeds and shichimi togarashi and serve.

1 tablespoon roughly chopped carrot

2 spring onions (scallions), chopped, plus extra for garnish

1 garlic clove

2 cm (¾ inch) piece ginger, chopped

500 g (1 lb 2 oz) boneless, skinless chicken thighs, chopped

2 teaspoons soy sauce

finely grated zest of 1 lemon

vegetable oil, for brushing

4 TSUKUNE CHICKEN MEATBALLS
(MAKES 6 SKEWERS)

Preheat a barbecue, chargrill pan or the grill (broiler) to high. If using wooden skewers, soak them in water for at least 10 minutes to prevent them from burning during cooking.

Put the carrot, spring onions, garlic and ginger in a food processor and pulse until chopped. Add the chicken, soy sauce and lemon zest and process until the meat is finely chopped. Lightly oil your hands and divide the meat into 18 portions. Roll into meatballs, then season all over with salt and pepper (to season the outside, not the mixture: the pepper makes it look good). Thread 3 meatballs onto each skewer, then brush with oil on all sides. Cook for 2 minutes on each side, then brush with the Teriyaki Sauce until thickly glazed.

6 very small red onions, halved

12 shiitake mushrooms, halved

12 thick asparagus spears, halved

vegetable oil, for brushing

5 VEGETABLES
(MAKES 12 SKEWERS)

Preheat a barbecue, chargrill pan or the grill (broiler) to high. If using wooden skewers, soak them in water for at least 10 minutes to prevent them from burning during cooking.

Thread the onion halves onto 4 skewers. Do the same with the other vegetables, then brush with oil on all sides and season well. Cook for 2 minutes on each side, then brush with the Teriyaki Sauce or the Miso Sauce until thickly glazed.

GET AHEAD The chicken meatballs can be rolled but not cooked and the sauces prepared the night before, then covered and refrigerated.

Granita is one of the easiest ways to make a frozen treat without an ice-cream maker. Lychees, ginger and grapefruit will soothe your palate with an icy pop of sweet and tart.

LYCHEE & GINGER GRANITA WITH RASPBERRIES

PREPARATION: 10 MINUTES, PLUS 3 HOURS FREEZING • COOKING: 10 MINUTES • SERVES: 4–6

200 g (7 oz) caster (superfine) sugar
70 g (2½ oz) piece ginger, peeled and sliced
800 g (1 lb 12 oz) tin lychees, drained, 175 ml (5½ fl oz/⅔ cup) of the juice reserved
juice of 2 limes
juice of 1 grapefruit

Raspberries and whipped cream or Greek-style yoghurt, to serve

Put the sugar, ginger and 250 ml (9 fl oz/1 cup) water in a saucepan. Stir over low heat until the sugar dissolves, then simmer for 8–10 minutes until syrupy. Remove from heat and discard the ginger. Stand until cool, then refrigerate until cold.

Put the drained lychees, reserved juice, ginger syrup and lime and grapefruit juices in a blender and process until smooth. Pour into a shallow dish and freeze until the outer edges of the granita set. Scrape with a fork to break up the ice crystals, then return to the freezer and repeat the scraping every 30 minutes until it is a gravel-like consistency. Serve the granita with fresh berries and a spoonful of soft whipped cream or Greek-style yoghurt.

GET AHEAD Once the granita is fully scraped you can freeze it again and keep frozen for 1 week. Thaw for 10 minutes before serving and break it up again with a large fork or use a potato masher.

EXTRAS & SIMPLE SIDES

ICEBERG LETTUCE WITH CARROT GINGER DRESSING
PREPARATION: 10 MINUTES • SERVES: 4

Blitz this tangy dressing in a blender to drizzle over crisp chunks of iceberg lettuce, or use it on any salad or raw vegetables.

½ head iceberg lettuce, cut into chunks
1 Lebanese (short) cucumber, cut into small chunks
10 cherry tomatoes, halved
4 spring onions (scallions), chopped

Carrot ginger dressing
2 teaspoons chopped carrot
1 teaspoon chopped ginger
1 French shallot, chopped
1 teaspoon caster (superfine) sugar
3 teaspoons soy sauce
1½ tablespoons rice vinegar
60 ml (2 fl oz/¼ cup) vegetable oil

To make the dressing, place all of the ingredients in a blender or food processor and process until smooth. Put the lettuce, cucumber, tomato and spring onion in a bowl and pour the dressing over just before serving.

GET AHEAD The dressing can be made the day before and stored in a screw-top glass jar. Assemble the salad and toss with the dressing just before serving.

GREEN BEANS WITH SESAME MISO SAUCE
PREPARATION: 15 MINUTES • COOKING: 5 MINUTES • SERVES: 4

Use this delicious sesame dressing for noodles, roasted eggplant (aubergine) and other vegetables.

250 g (9 oz) fine green beans, trimmed
1 teaspoon black sesame seeds, to serve

Sesame miso sauce
40 g (1½ oz/¼ cup) white sesame seeds
2 tablespoons soy sauce
2 tablespoons caster (superfine) sugar
1 tablespoon rice wine vinegar
1 tablespoon mirin (rice wine)
1 tablespoon sweet white miso (shiro miso)
  or other pale miso
1 tablespoon sesame oil

To make the sesame miso sauce, put the white sesame seeds in a small frying pan over low heat and dry-fry for 4–5 minutes until golden. Remove and grind in a mortar and pestle. Add all of the remaining ingredients and combine well.

Cook the beans in a large saucepan of lightly salted boiling water for 1 minute. Drain, rinse under cold running water and drain again. Pat dry with a tea towel (dish towel) and transfer to a platter.

Just before serving, pour the sesame miso dressing over the top and sprinkle with the black sesame seeds.

GET AHEAD The sauce and the blanched beans can be prepared earlier in the day, covered and refrigerated.

QUICK JAPANESE CUCUMBER PICKLES
PREPARATION: 10 MINUTES • MAKES: 3 CUPS

You can make any pickled vegetable with this marinade, so try carrots, cauliflower, celery, fennel, daikon or baby turnips.

3 Lebanese (short) or kirby cucumbers,
  cut into 5 mm (¼ inch) slices
2 teaspoons salt
125 ml (4 fl oz/½ cup) rice wine vinegar
100 g (3½ oz) caster (superfine) sugar
250 ml (9 fl oz/1 cup) warm water

Toss the cucumber with the salt in a bowl. Put the vinegar, sugar and water in another bowl and stir until the sugar is dissolved. Transfer the unrinsed cucumbers to a large sterilised glass jar or container (sterilising it in the dishwasher is fine) and pour the brine over. Cover and refrigerate for at least 1 day and up to 1 week before using.

KIMCHI

PREPARATION: 15 MINUTES, PLUS 2 HOURS SALTING AND 1 DAY STANDING •
FILLS: 500 ML (17 FL OZ/2 CUPS) CAPACITY JAR

You can buy kimchi, but when it's fresh with a firm bite to it, there is nothing better. This dish does have copious amounts of garlic, so don't be surprised to find vacant seats near you or people standing at a distance after you've eaten it.

1 head Chinese cabbage (wong bok)
2 tablespoons kosher salt or flaked sea salt
10 garlic cloves, finely chopped
1½ tablespoons finely chopped ginger
75 g (2¾ oz/⅓ cup) caster (superfine) sugar
1½ tablespoons fish sauce
1½ tablespoons light soy sauce
25 g (1 oz/¼ cup) gochugaru (Korean chilli powder)
150 g (5½ oz) daikon (white radish) or carrot,
   peeled and julienned
6 spring onions (scallions), sliced into 4 cm
   (1½ inch) pieces

Halve and core the cabbage, then cut into long strips. Cut these into 4 cm (1½ inch) pieces. Put the pieces in a large bowl and massage the salt into the cabbage. Stand for 2 hours or cover and refrigerate overnight if time permits. Rinse and drain the cabbage.

Combine the garlic, ginger, sugar, fish sauce, soy sauce, gochugaru and 2 tablespoons water in a large bowl. Add the cabbage, daikon and spring onions and combine with your hands (you might want to wear plastic gloves as the odours and colours can stay with you). Add a little more water if the sauce is too thick.

Pack into a large sterilised jar with a fitted lid or a sealable container. Refrigerate for at least 24 hours. After 1 day you can eat it, but the flavours will be a little stronger each day. Open the lid once a day to make sure everything is submerged in the liquid.

GET AHEAD Prepare kimchi up to 2 weeks in advance.

TIP There's no magic involved to prepare kimchi, but you do need to purchase the gochugaru (Korean chilli powder). The easiest way is online. To make kimchi the traditional way, tiny pink brined shrimp are used as the fermentation agent, but unless you have a Korean grocery store nearby they are tricky to get hold of. I've improvised with fish sauce, which is little less full on than the traditional method. Be sure to use a very tightly sealed container to store this, otherwise 'fermenting' odours will start to dominate your fridge.

SOUTH-EAST ASIA

IMPERIAL PORK
& HAPPY
PANCAKES

Hoi An is a magical Vietnamese city with old temples, colourful paper lanterns and quaint little bridges. The city's sophisticated cooks like to take a modern spin on old royal Hue cuisine and there aren't many experiences that could exceed a mouthful of this flaky hot spring roll, wrapped in fragrant herbs and dunked into tangy lime dipping sauce. The hot–cold sensations will make your mouth sing.

CRISPY PRAWN SPRING ROLLS WITH MINT & LETTUCE WRAPS

PREPARATION: 30 MINUTES • COOKING: 25 MINUTES • MAKES: 24 SPRING ROLLS

24 small spring roll wrappers
1 eggwhite, lightly beaten
vegetable oil, for deep-frying

Mint, coriander, basil and baby cos (gem) lettuce leaves, to serve
Chilli Lime Dipping Sauce (see page 227) and Sticky Cucumber Relish (see page 228), to serve

Prawn filling
1 small carrot, peeled and coarsely chopped
2 cm (¾ inch) piece ginger, peeled
3 small red Asian shallots, peeled
300 g (10½ oz) peeled raw prawns
25 g (1 oz) dried rice vermicelli
2 teaspoons fish sauce

Preheat the oven to 180°C (350°F) or 160°C (315°F) fan forced.

To make the filling, put the carrot, ginger and shallots in a food processor and process until finely chopped. Add the prawns and pulse until coarsely chopped, then transfer to a bowl. Soak the vermicelli in hot water for 5 minutes or until soft. Drain and chop into 2.5 cm (1 inch) lengths. Add to the prawn mixture with the fish sauce and mix well.

Lay a spring roll wrapper with one point towards you (so it looks like a diamond shape) on a work surface. Lightly brush the edges of the wrapper with a little eggwhite and place 1 tablespoon of the filling in the lower third of the wrapper. Bring the bottom corner up and over the filling, fold in the side corners and roll into a cigar shape. Brush the edges with a little more eggwhite and seal. Place the roll seam-side down on a tray lined with baking paper. Repeat with the remaining wrappers and filling.

Fill a wok or deep heavy-based saucepan to a depth of 6 cm (2½ inches) with vegetable oil and heat to 170°C (325°F). When a piece of bread dropped into the oil sizzles quickly, the oil is ready. Deep-fry 5 spring rolls at a time for 3–4 minutes until golden. Try not to let them touch each other while they are frying. Remove with tongs and drain on paper towel, then put them on a baking tray and keep warm in the oven while you cook the remainder. Serve with the lettuce and herbs for wrapping, with the Chilli Lime Dipping Sauce or Sticky Cucumber Relish in separate small bowls.

GET AHEAD Make the dipping sauce earlier in the day, but add the chilli close to serving. Prepare the rolls, lay them on a tray between sheets of baking paper and cover with plastic wrap. Refrigerate for up to 24 hours or freeze. If freezing the spring rolls, cook the frozen rolls without thawing in the hot oil but give them an extra minute longer to cook.

The ingenuity revealed in Vietnamese and Thai salads always astounds me. The pairing of meat and fruit is stunning and they're particularly refreshing for hot weather. You can use seafood, such as prawns (shrimp), in place of the salmon but practically anything will taste amazing with the creamy lime dressing, fried shallots and toasted coconut flakes.

CARAMELISED SALMON SALAD WITH COCONUT DRESSING

PREPARATION: 20 MINUTES • COOKING: 10 MINUTES • SERVES: 4

4 small salmon fillets with skin, about
   100 g (3½ oz) each
1 tablespoon soft brown sugar
100 g (3½ oz) thin green beans,
   trimmed
1 large ripe but firm mango, peeled
   and cut into 2 cm (¾ inch) strips
1 handful of mint leaves
1 handful of coriander (cilantro)
   leaves
25 g (1 oz/¼ cup) desiccated
   (shredded) coconut, toasted
1 red bird's eye chilli, thinly sliced
1 quantity Fried Shallots & Garlic
   (see page 227)
2 tablespoons roasted and coarsely
   chopped peanuts or cashews

Dressing
50 ml (1¾ fl oz) coconut cream
juice of 2 limes
3 teaspoons fish sauce
2 teaspoons soft brown sugar

Preheat the grill (broiler) on high. Season the salmon fillets on the flesh side with salt and freshly ground black pepper and lay on a baking tray, skin-side down. Combine the brown sugar with 1 teaspoon of water and brush over the fish, then grill for 7 minutes or until caramelised on the edges and cooked to your liking. Remove and set aside.

Meanwhile, cook the beans in a saucepan of lightly salted boiling water for 1 minute. Drain and refresh under cold running water, then pat dry with a tea towel (dish towel). Divide the beans and mango between four plates.

To make the dressing, combine all of the ingredients in a small bowl.

Break the salmon into pieces, discarding the skin, and divide among the plates. Scatter with herbs, toasted coconut, sliced chilli, fried shallots and garlic and the chopped nuts, then pour a little dressing over each plate and serve immediately.

GET AHEAD Make the dressing, toast the coconut and nuts, fry the shallots and garlic and blanch the beans earlier in the day. Cover everything and refrigerate. Assemble the salad and grill the salmon just before serving.

They say som tam is heaven on its own, but this salad of crisp unripe papaya ribbons and spicy lime dressing also creates the perfect base for seared prawns, sliced beef or sticky pork belly. The pounding of the ingredients is key; even though most of us don't own a Thai clay mortar and pestle you can improvise with a big bowl and the flat end of a rolling pin. Pounding infuses the flavour into the papaya and softens it. Three small bird's eye chillies will make your salad spicy but not eyeball-popping hot. Feel free to adjust the number to your liking.

GREEN PAPAYA & CARROT SALAD

PREPARATION: 30 MINUTES • SERVES 4 AS A SIDE

1 green papaya, about 400 g (14 oz),
    peeled
4 garlic cloves
3 small red chillies, sliced
1 large carrot, peeled and julienned
50 g (1¾ oz) baby green beans,
    halved
125 ml (4 fl oz/½ cup) lime juice
2 tablespoons firmly packed grated
    palm sugar (jaggery) or soft
    brown sugar
1½ tablespoons fish sauce
6 cherry tomatoes, halved
40 g (1½ oz/¼ cup) coarsely
    chopped roasted peanuts
    or cashews

PALM SUGAR

The crystallised sap of a palm tree, palm sugar is sold in plastic tubs at Asian grocery stores. It adds a caramel taste to dressings, curries and just about everything Thai or Vietnamese. Sometimes it can be rock hard, so heat it for a few seconds in a microwave to soften, then chop off a piece and grate it. It will dissolve much faster. Use soft brown sugar as a substitute if you can't get it. Be sure to refrigerate it after opening.

Cut the papaya in half lengthways and scrape out the seeds with a spoon. Using a julienne tool or a large grater, coarsely shred the flesh. If you're using a box grater, use it on the side of the sink to get long fat shreds of the papaya. Discard the inner part of the fruit and set aside the shredded green papaya.

Pound the garlic and chilli in a large mortar and pestle for 1 minute or until coarsely crushed (it should still have chunks and not be a paste). Add the papaya, carrot and beans and gently pound a little more. Add the lime juice, palm sugar and fish sauce and pound again for another minute. Add the tomato and taste to make sure it has enough fish sauce and sugar, it should be tangy, sweet and spicy. Place on a platter, scatter the nuts over the top and serve immediately.

For a meat-eaters' variation, serve with chunky pieces of Sticky Pork (see page 228.)

GET AHEAD Squeeze the limes, shred the papaya and carrot, and cut up the beans and tomatoes earlier in the day. Cover everything and refrigerate. Pound the salad just before serving.

When I was in Hanoi I was awestruck by the intense flavour of the chicken (clearly not battery-farmed). Something told me it was fresh when I could hear the roosters cock-a-doodle-dooing outside my hotel room. I never did get the name of this delectable dish, which originally had fried wings slathered in a spicy tamarind sauce with pickled chillies and shallots. I morphed it into seared boneless thighs to make a simple meal. Be sure to pick up corn-fed or free-range chicken as it makes a big difference.

CHICKEN WITH TAMARIND SAUCE, SHALLOTS & PICKLED CHILLIES

PREPARATION: 25 MINUTES, PLUS 1 HOUR MARINATING • COOKING: 25 MINUTES • SERVES: 4

8 boneless, skinless chicken thighs, quartered
60 ml (2 fl oz/¼ cup) fish sauce
2½ tablespoons sugar
2 garlic cloves, crushed
cornflour (cornstarch), for dusting
80 ml (2½ fl oz/⅓ cup) vegetable oil
2 red Asian shallots, thinly sliced into half moons
1 thumb-size red chilli, sliced and soaked in 2 tablespoons rice wine vinegar
2 tablespoons torn mint leaves
2 tablespoons coriander (cilantro) leaves

Fried Shallots & Garlic (see page 227), to serve

Tamarind sauce
1½ tablespoons tamarind purée
1 teaspoon finely grated garlic
juice of 2 limes
1½ tablespoons finely grated palm sugar (jaggery) or soft brown sugar
1 tablespoon fish sauce
2 teaspoons chilli flakes

Combine the chicken, fish sauce, sugar and garlic in a large bowl and season with black pepper. Cover and refrigerate for at least 1 hour, or overnight if time permits.

Meanwhile, to make the tamarind sauce, put all the ingredients in a small saucepan and stir over low heat for 5 minutes or until the sugar has dissolved. Remove from the heat and set aside.

Drain the chicken and pat dry with paper towel. Dust the chicken in cornflour and shake off the excess. Put two large frying pans over medium–high heat and add 2 tablespoons of vegetable oil to each pan. When the oil is nearly smoking, add the chicken and cook, in batches, for 3 minutes on each side. When the chicken is browned all over, reduce the heat to medium–low and cook, turning frequently, for another 5 minutes or until cooked through. Drain on paper towel.

Transfer the hot crisp chicken to a large serving platter. Spoon the tamarind sauce over the top, then scatter with the sliced shallots, pickled chilli and herbs. Top with Fried Shallots & Garlic.

GET AHEAD The day before, pickle the chilli, marinate the chicken, cover and refrigerate. Make the tamarind sauce earlier in the day. Cook the chicken just before serving.

Ask any Thai person for their version of green curry and you will get a completely different story each time. Being bordered by Malaysia, Laos and Myanmar (Burma), each region has its own influences, so the variations are endless. My paste is quick, easy and won't leave you sweating insanely from too many bird's eye chillies.

PRAWN GREEN CURRY WITH BAMBOO SHOOTS

PREPARATION: 20 MINUTES • COOKING: 15 MINUTES • SERVES: 4

400 ml (14 fl oz) coconut milk
1½ tablespoons grated palm sugar
   (jaggery) or soft brown sugar
45 ml (1½ fl oz) fish sauce
8 kaffir lime leaves
900 g (2 lb) large raw prawns
   (shrimp), peeled
100 g (3½ oz) green beans, halved
150 g (5½ oz) drained tinned bamboo
   shoots, sliced into thin strips
finely grated zest and juice of 2 limes
1 handful of Thai basil leaves
1 handful of coriander (cilantro)
   leaves

Steamed jasmine rice, to serve

Curry paste
8 green bird's eye chillies, stems
   removed, seeded, sliced
2 thumb-size green chillies, stems
   removed, seeded, sliced
1 tablespoon chopped galangal
1 large slice lime peel, pith removed,
   chopped
10 lemongrass stems, pale part only,
   finely chopped
4 kaffir lime leaves, finely chopped
15 g (½ oz) coriander (cilantro), roots
   and stems rinsed and chopped
   (reserve leaves for the main dish)
4 small red Asian shallots
6 garlic cloves
2 teaspoons kapi (fermented
   shrimp paste)

To make the curry paste, put all of the ingredients with 2 tablespoons of water and a good grind of black pepper in a blender and process until a fine paste forms.

Scoop out 2 tablespoons of the thicker coconut sediment from the tin of coconut milk, put it in a saucepan or wok and bring it to the boil over medium–high heat. Reduce the heat to low and simmer until the cream starts to split. Add the curry paste and stir for 5 minutes or until fragrant. Add the palm sugar and stir until dissolved, then add the remaining coconut milk, fish sauce and kaffir lime leaves. Bring to a simmer, then add the prawns and simmer for 5 minutes or until nearly cooked through.

Add the beans, bamboo shoots, lime zest and juice and cook for another 2 minutes, then add the Thai basil leaves and coriander leaves. Taste to see if it needs any extra fish sauce or sugar. Serve with steamed jasmine rice.

NOTE You can replace the prawns with the same quantity of sliced chicken breast or pork fillet for variety.

GET AHEAD Three days ahead you can make the curry paste and keep it covered and refrigerated. It also freezes well. Make the base for the curry with the coconut milk and other ingredients earlier in the day. Poach the meat or prawns in the curry base just before serving.

KAPI

This fermented shrimp paste is made from small salted shrimp that are dried in the sun and then pounded into a paste. The result is an extremely pungent and salty paste. As with fish sauce, it is hard to believe that something that smells so rank can make food taste so good. But once mixed with other ingredients, it contributes a savoury depth of flavour. Slot in extra fish sauce or 2 anchovies as a suitable replacement.

You will be happy indeed when you eat these amazing pancakes, called bánh xèo, from Hue, Vietnam. The rice flour makes a thick lacy pancake that is wrapped in chilled lettuce and stuffed with prawns, crisp bean sprouts and fragrant herbs. Dip it in sharp Chilli Lime Dipping Sauce (nuoc cham) for a burst of freshness. You can use two frying pans at once if you want to speed up the process of cooking. These can also be served as a snack. Cut the folded pancake into triangles and serve on baby cos leaves with the herbs, prawns and chilli and lime dipping sauce.

HAPPY PANCAKES WITH PRAWNS & LIME CHILLI SAUCE

PREPARATION: 20 MINUTES, PLUS 1 HOUR STANDING • COOKING: 10 MINUTES • SERVES: 4

130 g (4½ oz) rice flour
20 g (¾ oz) cornflour (cornstarch)
1 egg
1 teaspoon ground turmeric
75 ml (2¼ fl oz) coconut milk
1–2 tablespoons vegetable oil,
   for frying

2 heads baby cos (gem) lettuce,
   leaves separated, to serve
Lime wedges, to serve
Chilli Lime Dipping Sauce (see
   page 227) or Sticky Cucumber
   Relish (see page 228), to serve

Fillings
200 g (7 oz) cooked peeled prawns
   (shrimp)
4 large handfuls of fresh bean
   sprouts, trimmed
1 handful each of dill, mint, Thai basil
   and coriander (cilantro) leaves
4 spring onions (scallions), shredded

To make the pancakes, put the rice flour, cornflour, egg, turmeric and a pinch of salt in a large bowl. Add the coconut milk and 75 ml (2¼ fl oz) water and whisk until smooth. Set aside for 1 hour or cover and refrigerate for up to 12 hours.

Prepare the dipping sauce and fillings and set aside. It's best to chill the lettuce and herbs on a tray covered with wet paper towel so they are crisp when you serve them.

Heat two medium frying pans over medium–high heat. Put 2 teaspoons of vegetable oil in each pan. When hot, put 2 tablespoons of the pancake mixture in each pan and swirl to coat the base. Cook for 2–3 minutes until golden and crisp. Remove from the heat and place one-quarter of the fillings on one side. Fold the other side over and slide onto a plate. Repeat with the remaining batter and fillings. Serve immediately with the lettuce and lime wedges and a small bowl of Chilli Lime Dipping Sauce or Sticky Cucumber Relish for dipping.

GET AHEAD Make the batter and dipping sauce earlier in the day, then cover and refrigerate. Slice and chop all of the fillings and cover with damp paper towel and plastic wrap and keep chilled in the refrigerator.

In Hanoi, restaurants are dedicated solely to serving Vietnam's iconic national dish: pho. Little street stalls also abound, with the world's smallest plastic stools set out for you to sit on while you hunch over your steaming hot noodle soup. I've been told it's meant for breakfast, but people seem to eat it all day. If you truly want to recreate the real McCoy then making your own stock is imperative. I know that sounds like an almighty job, but your efforts will be rewarded.

SHORT-RIB BEEF & RICE NOODLE SOUP

PREPARATION: 20 MINUTES • COOKING: 4 HOURS 45 MINUTES • SERVES: 4–6

Broth

1.8 kg (4 lb) beef short ribs, brisket or oxtail

2 large pieces ginger, halved lengthways

2 onions, unpeeled, halved crossways

1 teaspoon salt

60 ml (2 fl oz/¼ cup) fish sauce

2½ tablespoons grated palm sugar (jaggery) or soft brown sugar

5 star anise

6 cloves

1 cinnamon stick

3 teaspoons fennel seeds

Preheat oven to 220°C (425°F) or 200°C (400°F) fan forced.

To make the broth, put the beef short ribs in a roasting tin and cook for 45 minutes or until browned. Drain the oil from the tin, then transfer the meat to a stockpot or large saucepan. Cover with 4 litres of cold water and bring to the boil.

While the broth is coming to the boil, preheat your grill (broiler). Put the ginger and onion on a baking tray and grill for 3–5 minutes each side until blackened. This adds a smoky taste to the broth. Peel the onion and discard the skin. Add the charred onion and ginger, salt and all of the remaining ingredients to the broth. Once it reaches the boil, reduce the heat to as low as possible, cover with a lid, leaving it slightly ajar, and simmer for 3–4 hours. It's important not to stir the stock or it will become cloudy so just leave it to bubble away slowly. Strain the broth through a fine sieve into a clean saucepan. Reserve the meat and discard the vegetables and spices. When cool enough to handle, pull the meat off the bones and discard the bones, sinew and fatty pieces. Pull the meat into small pieces and set aside.

Skim the excess fat off the broth, then bring to a gentle simmer. Taste the stock and add extra fish sauce or more sugar if needed. It should be slightly salty with a little tang.

Soup

300 g (10½ oz) beef sirloin or
    fillet steak
vegetable oil, for drizzling
300 g (10½ oz) thin dried rice
    noodles
1 small red onion, halved and thinly
    sliced into half moons
2 red chillies, sliced and soaked in
    2 tablespoons rice wine vinegar
4 large handfuls of trimmed
    bean sprouts
1 large handful of coriander (cilantro)
    leaves
1 large handful of mint leaves
1 large handful of Thai basil leaves

Sriracha and lime wedges, to serve

SRIRACHA

*Made from red chillies, garlic, vinegar,
sugar and salt, this fiery sauce can be used
as a condiment with soups, fried food and
meat. It graces most Thai and Vietnamese
restaurant tables and can be purchased
from most supermarkets. Originally from
Thailand, it's now used all over Asia.*

Making the seared steak to serve is traditional but if you want to save time you can enjoy the soup with just the short rib meat. Lightly oil and season the steak and cook on a barbecue or chargrill pan preheated to high heat for 2 minutes on each side for medium rare (depending on the thickness of the meat). Stand for 10 minutes, then cut against the grain into thin slices.

While the beef is resting, soak the rice noodles in boiling water for 5 minutes or until al dente. Drain and divide between four to six serving bowls. Divide the beef rib meat between the bowls and ladle 2–3 cups of broth over the top. Top with a few slices of grilled steak. Serve the onion, pickled chilli, bean sprouts, herbs, sriracha and lime wedges in small separate bowls to allow each person to garnish their own soup.

GET AHEAD Make the stock up to 3 days ahead and store, covered, in the refrigerator. Remove any solidified fat before reheating.

Until recently, making the perfect pad Thai had eluded me. I tried numerous renditions but it never had the wow factor. A talented chef called Alima, from Krabi, showed me how it was done. Two important light bulb moments happened: firstly, you can't make a big batch in one wok, because it goes soggy (most Thais cook individual portions); secondly, the noodles should be firm when they go into the wok. The high heat and smaller quantity of noodles finish the cooking and create the ultimate texture. Have all the ingredients prepared and close by before you start cooking.

PERFECT PAD THAI
PREPARATION: 15 MINUTES, PLUS 20 MINUTES SOAKING • COOKING: 20 MINUTES • SERVES: 4

250 g (9 oz) dried rice stick noodles
2 tablespoons vegetable oil
300 g (10½ oz) raw prawns (shrimp), peeled and deveined
2 eggs
115 g (4 oz/1 cup) bean sprouts
2 tablespoons finely chopped pickled turnip (optional)
small handful of chives or garlic chives, snipped into 2.5 cm (1 inch) pieces

Lime wedges, roasted and coarsely ground peanuts and coriander (cilantro) leaves, to serve

Pad Thai sauce
1 tablespoon vegetable oil
3 garlic cloves, finely chopped
3 bird's eye chillies (or 1 thumb-size red chilli), stems removed, finely chopped
2½ tablespoons grated palm sugar (jaggery) or soft brown sugar
90 g (3 oz) tamarind purée mixed with 50 ml (1¾ fl oz) water
50 ml (1¾ fl oz) fish sauce
2 teaspoons light soy sauce

Break the noodles into 15 cm (6 inch) pieces and put them in a large bowl. Cover with warm water and stand for 20 minutes. They should soften, but they will still be fairly firm when you start to cook them.

Meanwhile, to make the pad Thai sauce, heat the vegetable oil in a wok over low heat. Add the garlic and chilli and stir for 1 minute. Add the remaining ingredients and stir for 1 minute or until the sugar dissolves. Pour into a small bowl and clean the wok.

You can only make 2 portions at a time in the wok, but it doesn't take long to cook and is better than crowding the wok. Heat the wok over high heat and add 1 tablespoon of vegetable oil. When the oil is nearly smoking, add half the prawns and toss for 1 minute or until pink. Push the prawns to the side and crack an egg into the centre of the wok. Stir so that it scrambles. Add half the bean sprouts and chopped pickled turnip, if using, and stir for 1 minute. Drain the noodles and add half to the wok with half the sauce and half the chives. Using two long spoons, toss the noodles constantly for 3–4 minutes or until heated through.

Divide the pad Thai between two plates, then wipe the pan clean and repeat with the remaining ingredients. Scatter with peanuts and coriander and serve with lime wedges.

GET AHEAD Make the sauce the day before, cover and refrigerate. One hour before cooking, prepare the remaining components.

PICKLED TURNIP
You can find this yellow-hued ingredient in Asian grocery stores. It is usually sold whole in plastic bags or chopped in jars. It adds a subtle sour taste to stir-fries or noodle dishes and is used in Chinese, Malay and Thai cooking. You can substitute with Japanese or Korean pickled radish or even chopped pickled ginger. Once you get over its strangeness you will see the benefit it adds. Don't fret if you can't find it, simply leave it out of the recipe.

Tom yum goong (hot and sour soup) and tom kha gai (chicken, coconut and galangal) are both legendary Thai soups and it was tortuous to decide which to feature in this book. But after slurping down the best bowl ever in a street stall in Bangkok I realised I could have both. Basically, this is tom yum with coconut cream: the best of both worlds. If you want to bulk this out into a meal on its own, add some rice or noodles.

HOT & SOUR COCONUT PRAWN & PINEAPPLE SOUP

PREPARATION: 25 MINUTES • COOKING: 40 MINUTES • SERVES: 4–6

6 lemongrass stems, pale part only, finely chopped

3 red shallots

3 garlic cloves

20 g (¾ oz) piece galangal, peeled and chopped

1 small bunch coriander (cilantro), roots and stems washed well, leaves reserved

1 litre (35 fl oz/4 cups) vegetable or chicken stock

8 kaffir lime leaves

250 ml (9 fl oz/1 cup) coconut cream

1 tablespoon roasted chilli paste (nam prik pao) or 3 chopped bird's eye chillies

2 tablespoons tamarind purée

2 tablespoons lime juice

1 tablespoon finely grated palm sugar (jaggery) or soft brown sugar

2 tablespoons fish sauce

10 small chestnut mushrooms, halved

300 g (10½ oz) large raw prawns (shrimp), butterflied

200 g (7 oz) fresh pineapple, cut into 3 cm (1¼ inch) pieces

Sliced red chillies, to serve (optional)

Put the lemongrass, shallots, garlic, galangal, and coriander roots and stems in a mortar and pestle and pound until coarsely chopped. Transfer the paste to a large saucepan, add the stock and 4 of the kaffir lime leaves. Bring to a simmer over medium heat and cook for 30 minutes. Strain the stock through a fine sieve into a clean saucepan and discard the solids.

Add the coconut cream, roasted chilli paste, tamarind purée, lime juice, palm sugar, fish sauce and mushrooms. Bring to a gentle simmer, then add the prawns, pineapple and the remaining kaffir lime leaves. Simmer for 3–4 minutes or until the mushrooms and prawns are just cooked. Ladle into bowls and serve sprinkled with the chilli, if using, and reserved coriander leaves.

GET AHEAD The soup base can be made up to the straining step 1 day in advance. Continue with the remainder of the recipe just before serving.

NAM PRIK PAO

This is a Thai chilli paste made with dried chillies, garlic, shallots, dried shrimp, tamarind, palm sugar and fish sauce. It adds a spicy depth to soups, stir-fries and fried rice dishes. It is available from Asian grocery stores. You can also substitute Chinese roasted chilli oil sediment (see page 151).

The stir-fries of Thailand are often forgotten, as the curries get centre stage. Most stir-fries take less than half an hour to prepare and have a lighter finish than their Chinese cousins. The use of both basil and fish sauce in this dish give it that Thai signature. You can buy fresh peppercorns from your local Asian grocery store, but mostly I use bottled and they are fine. Their heat sneaks up on you, so don't add too many.

THAI GREEN PEPPERCORN CHICKEN WITH BASIL & GREEN BEANS

PREPARATION: 20 MINUTES • COOKING: 15 MINUTES • SERVES: 4

500 g (1 lb 2 oz) boneless, skinless chicken thighs
1 thumb-size green chilli, halved
3 garlic cloves
1 tablespoon vegetable oil
1 onion, halved and sliced into half moons
100 g (3½ oz) baby green beans, cut into 4 cm (1½ inch) pieces
60 ml (2 fl oz/¼ cup) dark soy sauce
1½ tablespoons fish sauce
1½ tablespoons oyster sauce
juice of 1 lime
3 teaspoons fresh or brined green peppercorns
large handful of Thai basil leaves (or use regular basil)

Steamed jasmine rice, to serve

DARK SOY SAUCE

Less salty, thicker and with more molasses flavour than Chinese soy sauce, dark soy sauce is best for stir-fries. The heat brings out its flavour and it adds volume to sauces without the excess salt.

Cut the chicken into bite-size pieces. Deseed one chilli half, put it with the garlic in a mortar and pestle and pound into a rough paste.

Heat half the oil in a wok or large frying pan over medium heat. Cook the chicken, in batches, for 7–8 minutes until golden. Add the chilli and garlic paste and the remaining oil and stir-fry for 1–2 minutes. Add the onion and beans and cook for another 2 minutes. Add the combined sauces and lime juice and stir-fry for another minute or until sticky. Remove from the heat, add the peppercorns and basil and toss to combine. Serve immediately with steamed jasmine rice and the remaining chilli half, thinly sliced.

GET AHEAD Pound the chilli and garlic, and chop and stir-fry the chicken pieces earlier in the day, then cool, cover and refrigerate. Continue with the remainder of the recipe just before serving.

Charcoal, sugar, pork ... what's not to like? The streets of Hanoi are packed with hawkers crouched over tiny charcoal braziers turning little sticks of tantalising caramel pork. The liquid caramel glaze is the cornerstone of Vietnamese cooking, not just for grilling but for stews, fish and more. Whip up some of this insanely good pork for noodles (bun cha) or to fill the famous bánh mì baguettes.

IMPERIAL PORK TWO WAYS: BUN CHA OR BÁNH MÌ

PREPARATION: 20 MINUTES • COOKING: 10 MINUTES • SERVES: 4–6

1 garlic clove
3 small red Asian shallots
4 lemongrass stems, pale part only, finely chopped
500 g (1 lb 2 oz) minced (ground) pork
1 tablespoon fish sauce
45 g (1½ oz) soft brown sugar
vegetable oil, for brushing

Put the garlic, shallots and lemongrass in a blender or mortar and pestle and process or pound until finely chopped. Transfer to a bowl, then add the pork, fish sauce, 1 tablespoon of the sugar and a good grind of black pepper. Combine well, then divide the mixture into 18 portions and shape into balls. Flatten each ball slightly, then place on a heatproof metal rack and brush with oil.

Put the remaining sugar with 1 tablespoon of water in a small saucepan and stir over low heat until melted.

Preheat a barbecue, chargrill or a grill (broiler) to high. Cook the patties on one side for 2 minutes or until golden. Turn and brush the cooked side with the caramel mixture. Cook for another 2 minutes or until golden and crisp, then remove from the heat and brush with a little more caramel. Two ways of serving the Imperial Pork are given on the next page.

GET AHEAD The pork patties can be made up to 2 days beforehand and stored on trays between sheets of baking paper, then covered with plastic wrap. Freeze or refrigerate. Thaw in the refrigerator. Earlier in the day you can grill the patties so they are underdone. Put them on a baking tray, cover with foil, then finish them off in a 200°C (400°F) fan forced oven for 5 minutes. Drizzle with caramel just before eating.

CONTINUED

IMPERIAL PORK TWO WAYS:
BUN CHA OR BÁNH MÌ (CONTINUED)

250 g (9 oz) dried rice vermicelli
   noodles
1 quantity grilled imperial pork
   patties
1 handful of dill
1 handful of mint leaves
1 handful of coriander (cilantro)
   leaves
1 handful of Thai basil leaves
Fried Shallots & Garlic (see page 227)
   and Chilli Lime Dipping Sauce
   (see page 227)

1 PORK NOODLE SALAD: BUN CHA
PREPARATION: 10 MINUTES • SERVES: 4–6

Put the noodles in a bowl, cover with warm water and soak for
3–5 minutes or until al dente, then drain. Using kitchen scissors,
cut the noodles into shorter pieces and divide them among
4–6 bowls. Top with grilled pork patties, a selection of herbs,
Pickled Carrots and a sprinkling of Fried Shallots & Garlic. Serve
with the Chilli Lime Dipping Sauce to pour over.

4–6 small baguettes
mayonnaise, for spreading
1 quantity imperial pork patties
2 Lebanese (short) cucumbers, sliced
   into ribbons with a vegetable peeler
1 handful of coriander (cilantro)
   leaves
1 handful of mint leaves
1 handful of Thai basil leaves
1 quantity Pickled Carrots (see
   page 226), or 2 carrots, peeled
   and julienned

Sriracha, to serve

2 PORK BAGUETTES: BÁNH MÌ
PREPARATION: 10 MINUTES • SERVES: 4–6

Split the baguettes open down the centre. Spread with
mayonnaise, then fill with 3–4 grilled pork patties, cucumber
ribbons, a bit of each herb and a little pickled or fresh carrot.
Add sriracha to taste. Serve with plenty of napkins.

With influences from India, Thailand and China, Malaysian food is a glorious mash-up of complex flavours. This exotic coconut marinade is dreamy on any meat or fish.

MALAY GRILLED COCONUT FISH WITH LIME LEAVES & CUCUMBER RELISH

PREPARATION: 15 MINUTES, PLUS 30 MINUTES MARINATING • COOKING: 15 MINUTES • SERVES: 4–6

750 g (1 lb 10 oz) skinless thick white fish fillet (halibut, redfish, barramundi cod or salmon)
15 kaffir lime leaves
1 tablespoon vegetable oil

Steamed rice and Sticky Cucumber Relish (see page 228), to serve

Marinade
3 lemongrass stems, pale part only, chopped
5 cm (2 inch) piece galangal or ginger, peeled and chopped
2 garlic cloves
2 red Asian shallots
1 thumb-size red chilli, halved, seeded, roughly chopped
1 bunch coriander (cilantro), roots and stems rinsed, leaves reserved for serving
1½ tablespoons fish sauce
finely grated zest of 1 lime
1 teaspoon mild curry powder
200 ml (7 fl oz) coconut cream

To make the marinade, put all of the ingredients in a food processor or blender and process until smooth.

Cut the fish into 5 cm (2 inch) pieces. Put the pieces in a non-metallic shallow container and pour the marinade over. Cover and refrigerate for 30–60 minutes. If using wooden skewers, soak them in water for at least 15 minutes to prevent them from burning during cooking.

Alternately thread the fish pieces and kaffir lime leaves onto the skewers, then brush all over with vegetable oil. Cook the fish skewers on a preheated barbecue or chargrill or under a grill (broiler) on high heat for 2–3 minutes on each side until golden at the edges and just cooked through. Serve with steamed rice, chopped reserved coriander leaves and Sticky Cucumber Relish.

GET AHEAD Make the Sticky Cucumber Relish, blend the marinade and cut up the fish earlier in the day, then cover and refrigerate. Add the marinade no more than 1 hour before grilling.

This speciality from Isan—a northeastern region of Thailand—is found on practically every street corner in Bangkok and especially at the night markets. Wafts of garlic and lemongrass float in the air as they grill and brush the chicken pieces until they are lacquered and lush. Typically it is served on sticks (often with the clawed feet still on) so you can eat it without forks. But don't stop at poultry, try the glaze on grilled beef, fish or pork.

KAI YANG WITH CHILLI DIPPING SAUCE

PREPARATION: 20 MINUTES, PLUS 5 HOURS MARINATING • COOKING: 25 MINUTES • SERVES: 4–6

4 spatchcocks (poussins)
6 lemongrass stems, pale part only, finely chopped
2 thumb-size red chillies, sliced
5 garlic cloves
2 tablespoons chopped coriander (cilantro) roots or stems
60 ml (2 fl oz/¼ cup) fish sauce
100 g (3½ oz) grated palm sugar (jaggery) or soft brown sugar

Steamed rice, Chilli Lime Dipping Sauce (see page 227) or Sticky Cucumber Relish (see page 228) or Tamarind sauce (see page 205), to serve

GET AHEAD Marinate the chicken up to 24 hours ahead. Grill just before serving. If using the tamarind sauce or cucumber relish, they can be made 3 days before, although you should keep the cucumbers and shallots separate until just before serving.

Using poultry scissors, cut down the sides of the backbone of each spatchcock. Remove the backbone and flatten the birds.

Put the lemongrass, chilli, garlic, and coriander roots or stems in a mortar and pestle and pound until coarsely chopped. Alternatively, chop by hand. Transfer to a small bowl. Add the fish sauce and 1½ tablespoons of the sugar and combine well. Put two spatchcock each in large resealable plastic bags and pour half of the marinade into each bag. Alternatively, put all the spatchcocks in a shallow container and pour over the marinade. Seal or cover and refrigerate for at least 5 hours or overnight if time permits.

Prepare a barbecue or chargrill. It is best to cook this over indirect heat, so set up a drip pan between the hot coals or turn off the middle burners if using gas: that way you won't have flame-ups as fat drips down, and the spatchcock will cook evenly.

While the barbecue or chargrill is heating, put the remaining sugar and 2 tablespoons of water in a small bowl and stir until it has dissolved.

Cook the spatchcock for 10 minutes on one side, then turn and brush with the palm sugar glaze. Cook for another 10 minutes, then flip over and glaze again. Cook for another 4–5 minutes, continuing to brush with the glaze, until the spatchcock is cooked through and is golden and crisp on the edges.

Alternatively, the spatchcock can be roasted on a large baking tray in a 200°C (400°F) or 180°C (350°F) fan forced oven for 35–40 minutes until golden.

Remove from the heat and stand for 5 minutes, then cut the spatchcocks into pieces and place on a large platter. Serve with steamed rice, Chilli Lime Dipping Sauce, Sticky Cucumber Relish or Tamarind sauce.

It's not easy to find a thrilling dessert to cap off a South–East Asian meal: you want something easy and fresh and perhaps a little sinful. This simple tropical fruit crisp delivers just the thing, with a tasty, buttery coconut crumble. Any fruit can be slotted in, so if you want to add peaches, plums or berries, just use the same total weight of fruit.

TROPICAL FRUIT CRISP WITH COCONUT & CASHEW CRUMBLE

PREPARATION: 15 MINUTES • COOKING: 40 MINUTES • SERVES: 4–6

4 small ripe but firm mangoes, peeled
   and cut into 5 cm (2 inch) pieces
100 g (3½ oz) pineapple cut into 6 cm
   (2½ inch) pieces
4 passionfruit, pulp spooned out
2½ tablespoons caster (superfine)
   sugar
2 teaspoons cornflour (cornstarch)
1 teaspoon vanilla bean paste or
   natural vanilla extract

Ice cream, to serve

Coconut and cashew crumble
35 g (1¼ oz/¼ cup) plain
   (all-purpose) flour
2 tablespoons soft brown sugar
50 g (1¾ oz) cold unsalted butter,
   chopped
30 g (1 oz/⅓ cup) desiccated
   (shredded) coconut
2 tablespoons chopped cashew nuts

Preheat the oven to 190°C (375°F) or 170°C (325°F) fan forced.

Put the mango, pineapple and passionfruit pulp in a shallow baking dish, about 20 x 30 cm (8 x 10 inch). Add the sugar, cornflour and vanilla and toss gently.

To make the crumble mixture, put all of the ingredients in a bowl and rub the butter into the flour until the mixture resembles coarse breadcrumbs. Spread the crumble over the fruit and bake for 40 minutes or until golden and bubbling. Serve warm with ice cream.

GET AHEAD The crumble can be made 6 hours before cooking, then covered and refrigerated. Bake up to 1 hour before eating.

EXTRAS & SIMPLE SIDES

PICKLED CARROTS
PREPARATION: 10 MINUTES • COOKING: 5 MINUTES • MAKES: 1 CUP

Pickled carrot adds another taste layer to báhn mì rolls or bun cha noodles.

1 tablespoon fish sauce
2 tablespoons rice vinegar
juice of 1 lime
1 tablespoon caster (superfine) sugar
2 carrots, peeled and julienned

Put all of the ingredients except the carrot in a saucepan over low heat and stir until the sugar dissolves. Bring to the boil, then remove from the heat. Stir in the carrot, then pour the mixture into a bowl. Stand until cool, then refrigerate for at least 1 hour. To serve, drain the carrot.

GET AHEAD Leave the carrots to marinate for at least 1 hour and up to 3 days.

FRIED SHALLOTS & GARLIC

PREPARATION: 5 MINUTES • COOKING: 10 MINUTES

Although this might sometimes seem like a bridge too far, it's what really makes South–East Asian food special. The nutty salty taste and crunch add bags of flavour to any salad, curry or noodles.

500 ml (17 fl oz/2 cups) vegetable oil, for frying
6 small golden or red shallots, very thinly sliced
2 tablespoons plain (all-purpose) flour
2 garlic cloves, very thinly sliced

Pour the vegetable oil into a wok or saucepan so that it is about 10 cm (4 inches) deep, and warm over medium heat.

Combine the shallots and flour in a bowl, then transfer to a sieve and shake off the excess flour. The oil is ready when you put in a shallot and it sizzles. You don't want the oil too hot or they will burn and taste bitter. Gently fry the shallots for 5 minutes or until golden. Remove with a slotted spoon, drain on paper towel and sprinkle with salt. Add the sliced garlic to the oil (you don't need to dust it in flour) and cook for 1–2 minutes or until golden. Remove with the slotted spoon and drain on paper towel, then sprinkle with salt.

GET AHEAD The shallots and garlic can be fried, drained and salted on the morning of serving. Store in an airtight container.

CHILLI LIME DIPPING SAUCE (NUOC CHAM)

PREPARATION: 15 MINUTES • MAKES: ABOUT ¾ CUP

This dipping sauce is on every table in Vietnam. The Thais make theirs a bit sharper with less water but it's equally wonderful.

2 garlic cloves, peeled
2 cm (¾ inch) piece ginger, peeled
2 tablespoons grated palm sugar (jaggery)
  or caster (superfine) sugar
2 tablespoons hot water
2 tablespoons fish sauce
125 ml (4 fl oz/½ cup) lime juice
1 red chilli, thinly sliced

Pound the garlic, ginger and sugar in a mortar and pestle until a fine paste forms. Scrape into a small bowl, then add the remaining ingredients. Don't add the chilli too far in advance of serving, as the sauce gets too hot.

GET AHEAD The dipping sauce can be made 2 days ahead and refrigerated. The longer the chilli stays in the sauce, the hotter it becomes so add them at the last minute if you prefer less heat.

STICKY CUCUMBER RELISH

PREPARATION: 10 MINUTES • COOKING: 10 MINUTES • MAKES: 1½ CUPS

Use this refreshing dipping sauce for fried food, grilled meat or noodles.

2 garlic cloves
2 long red chillies, seeded and chopped
200 ml (7 fl oz) rice vinegar
200 g caster (superfine) sugar
2 teaspoons fish sauce
juice of 1 lime
1 tablespoon finely chopped red Asian shallot
50 g (1¾ oz) Lebanese (short) cucumber, finely chopped

Put the garlic and chilli in a mortar and pestle and pound into a paste. Scrape into a saucepan, then add the vinegar, sugar and a pinch of salt. Stir over medium heat until the sugar dissolves, then simmer for 6–8 minutes or until reduced and syrupy. Remove from the heat, add the fish sauce and stand until cool. Stir in the lime juice, shallot and cucumber.

GET AHEAD The sauce can be made 3 days ahead, then covered and refrigerated. Leave the cucumbers and shallots separate until serving so they are crisp. make separate recipe in extras:

STICKY PORK

PREPARATION: 10 MINUTES • COOKING: 1 HOUR 45 MINUTES • SERVES 4 WITH A SALAD

Serve this delicious glazed pork with a crisp salad or noodle dish such as the Green Papaya & Carrot Salad (see page 202).

1 kg (2 lb 4 oz) rindless pork shoulder or belly
2 teaspoons vegetable oil
250 ml (9 fl oz/1 cup) water
200 g (7 oz) soft brown sugar
60 ml (2 fl oz/¼ cup) fish sauce
1½ tablespoons soy sauce
2 tablespoons rice vinegar
5 star anise
2 teaspoons Chinese five spice

Preheat the oven to 180°C (350°F) or 160°C (315°F) fan forced.

Cut the pork into 4 cm (1½ inch) pieces. Heat the vegetable oil in a large heavy-based frying pan and brown the pork on all sides.

Transfer the pork to a large roasting tin with all of the remaining ingredients. Cover the tin tightly with foil and roast for 30 minutes. Remove the foil, increase the heat to 220°C (425°F) or 200°C (400°F) fan forced, and cook for another hour or until the sauce is completely syrupy. You will need to keep turning the pork every 15 minutes or so. Cool slightly, then slice the sticky pork into smaller pieces and serve.

PASSAGE TO INDIA

CHAI &
ROTI

Indian chaat are crispy snacks that involve a wicked trio of sweet, sour and salty tastes. The translation is 'to lick', so you get the picture. Chaat wallahs comb the beaches of Mumbai hawking little dishes of bhel puri. The base is usually chopped potatoes or chickpeas, drizzled with tamarind and coriander chutneys and sprinkled with crisp Bombay mix. Serve it up with poppadoms and icy cold beer.

BHEL PURI WITH POTATOES & GREEN CHUTNEY
PREPARATION: 30 MINUTES • COOKING: 20 MINUTES • SERVES: 4–6 AS A SNACK

400 g (14 oz) waxy potatoes,
    unpeeled
3 roma (plum) tomatoes, halved,
    seeded and chopped
1 small red onion, finely chopped
60 ml (2 fl oz/¼ cup) Date & Tamarind
    Dipping Sauce (see page 254)
60 ml (2 fl oz/¼ cup) Coriander
    Chutney (see page 255)
60 ml (2 fl oz/¼ cup) plain
    Greek-style yoghurt
3 large handfuls of sev mamra
    (see Note) or Bombay mix
chaat masala, for sprinkling
    (optional)

Poppadoms or Naan (see page 257),
    to serve

CHAAT MASALA

Sprinkle this spice mix on salads or curries just before serving to impart a sour astringent taste. Amchoor powder, the dominant sour ingredient, is dried ground mango. It's mixed with ground cumin, coriander, fennel, black salt, peppercorns, asafoetida, ginger, dried mint and ajowan seeds. You can buy good quality mixes of this from spice shops and online. Be sure to purchase in small quantities so it's fresh when you use it.

Put the potatoes in a saucepan of lightly salted cold water. Bring to the boil, then simmer until knife tender but not mushy. Drain, then return to the pan and gently shake over low heat for 30 seconds to dry out. When cool enough to handle, peel and set aside to cool.

Cut the cooled potatoes into 1 cm (⅜ inch) pieces, then place on a serving platter. Scatter with the tomato and onion, then drizzle with the Date & Tamarind Dipping Sauce, Coriander Chutney and the yoghurt. Sprinkle with the sev mamra or Bombay mix and the chaat masala, if using.

Serve immediately with poppadoms or naan bread.

NOTE Sev mamra is a snack mix of puffed rice, chickpea noodles and peanuts. You can also use a combination of Bombay mix with Rice Bubbles (Rice Krispies).

GET AHEAD Boil, peel and chop the potatoes earlier in the day and make both the dipping sauce and the chutney. Up to 2 hours before serving, assemble the potatoes, tomato and onion, then cover and refrigerate. Top with the dipping sauce and chutney, yoghurt and sev mamra just before serving.

Samosas are sold kerbside in most of India's regions, stuffed with spiced potatoes or minced lamb. Making your own dough gives them an ultracrisp pastry but you can use 20 small spring roll wrappers if you find making your own pastry a bridge too far. It's really worth doing and if you have a food processor it's no more difficult than making shortcrust (pie) pastry.

PEA & POTATO SAMOSAS
PREPARATION: 1 HOUR, PLUS 20 MINUTES STANDING • COOKING: 55 MINUTES • MAKES: 20 SMALL SAMOSAS

250 g (9 oz/1⅔ cups) plain
   (all-purpose) flour
½ teaspoon baking powder
2 tablespoons vegetable oil
1 teaspoon salt
625 ml (21½ fl oz/2½ cups) vegetable
   or peanut (groundnut) oil, for frying

Filling
200 g (7 oz) floury potato
1½ tablespoons vegetable oil
1 small onion, finely chopped
1 garlic clove, finely chopped
3 teaspoons finely grated ginger
1 thumb-size green chilli, seeded and
   finely chopped
1 teaspoon curry powder
1 teaspoon cumin seeds
1 teaspoon amchoor powder
   (optional)
150 g (5½ oz) fresh or frozen peas
small handful of coriander (cilantro)
   leaves, chopped

To make the filling, cook the potato in lightly salted boiling water until knife tender. Drain, then peel and cut into small pieces and mash slightly.

Heat the oil in a frying pan over low to medium heat. Add the onion, garlic, ginger and chilli, season with salt and pepper and cook for 7–8 minutes until soft. Add the spices and stir for 2–3 minutes until fragrant. Add the potato, peas and coriander and toss to combine well. Remove from the heat, transfer to a bowl and stand until cool.

Meanwhile, put the flour, baking powder, vegetable oil and salt in a food processor and pulse until the mixture resembles coarse sand. (Alternatively, combine the ingredients by hand in a bowl.) Add 125 ml (4 fl oz/½ cup) warm water. If the dough appears too dry, add a little extra water. Knead on a lightly floured work surface for 2–3 minutes to make a smooth ball. Wrap in plastic wrap and stand at room temperature for 20 minutes.

Date & Tamarind Dipping Sauce
(see page 254), Mint, Green Chilli
& Yoghurt Dipping Sauce (see
page 254) or Fresh Mango Chutney
(see page 255), to serve

AMCHOOR POWDER

*This is dried ground mango with a piquant,
citrus-like flavour. It adds a sour note to
salads or curries. Most online spice shops
or Indian grocery stores carry it.*

To assemble the samosas, divide the dough into 10 pieces.
Roll each piece on a lightly floured work surface into a circle
about 12 cm (4½ inch) in diameter, then cut it in half to make two
semicircles. Take the corners of one semicircle, bring the straight
edges together and overlap them slightly to make a cone. Seal
with a dab of water. Spoon 1 tablespoon of cooled filling into the
cone and moisten the curved edges lightly with water before
sealing tightly.

Heat the oil in a wok or heavy-based saucepan to 190°C
(375°F). When a piece of bread dropped into the oil sizzles
instantly, the oil is ready. Fry the samosas, 3–4 at a time, for
4 minutes or until golden and crisp. Drain on paper towel and
serve with the dipping sauces or the chutney.

GET AHEAD The samosas can be assembled and stored on a tray
between sheets of baking paper and covered in plastic wrap.
Fry just before serving. They can be frozen in a single layer, then
transferred to an airtight container and kept frozen for about a
month. Thaw in the refrigerator before frying.

Bhajis are one of the many kinds of pakora, vegetables deep-fried in a spiced chickpea flour batter. The chickpea flour makes a blistering crisp coating and tastes heavenly dipped into cool minty yoghurt sauce. You can use any vegetables, prawns or even bite-size pieces of firm fish.

RED ONION BHAJI
PREPARATION: 10 MINUTES • COOKING: 15 MINUTES • SERVES: 4–6 AS A SNACK

50 g (1¾ oz) chickpea flour (besan)

50 g (1¾ oz/⅓ cup) plain
  (all-purpose) flour

½ teaspoon baking powder

¼ teaspoon cumin seeds

¼ teaspoon ground turmeric

¼ teaspoon chilli powder

¼ teaspoon salt

2 large red onions, 1 finely chopped,
  1 halved and thinly sliced

500 ml (17 fl oz/2 cups) peanut
  (groundnut) or vegetable oil,
  for frying

Mint, Green Chilli & Yoghurt Dipping
  Sauce (see page 254), to serve

Put the combined flours, baking powder and spices in a bowl and combine well. Whisk in 125 ml (4 fl oz/½ cup) of water and combine until a thick smooth batter forms. Add the onions and stir until well coated.

Heat the peanut oil in a wok or heavy-based saucepan to 180°C (350°F) or until a little of the batter dropped in the oil sizzles quickly. If the oil is too hot, the bhaji will burn before the onions are cooked, so keep the heat steady. The first ones will cook the fastest, then the oil will go down in temperature so adjust it as you cook. Place tablespoons of the mixture into the oil, 4–5 at a time, and cook for 3–4 minutes until golden and crisp. Drain on paper towel and serve hot with the Mint, Green Chilli & Yoghurt Dipping Sauce.

GET AHEAD The dipping sauce can be made the day before, then cover and refrigerat. The fritters can be fried 3 hours ahead, kept covered at room temperature, then reheated in a 200°C (400°F) or 180°C (350°F) fan forced oven for 5 minutes. They are better freshly fried but they do reheat extremely well.

Bengalis are renowned for their love of mustard seeds. Both the seeds and oil are used prevalently in their cooking. My friend Rita, who grew up there, made this as part of a delicious lunch with warm naan bread. The pungent oil adds a nutty flavour to the silky eggplant and the whole spices add delicious pops of texture.

BENGALI SMOKED EGGPLANT DIP

PREPARATION: 10 MINUTES • COOKING: 15 MINUTES • SERVES: 4–6

2 large eggplants (aubergines)

2 tablespoons Greek-style yoghurt

1 small red onion, finely chopped

1 thumb-size green chilli, seeded and finely chopped

small handful of coriander (cilantro) leaves, chopped

1 teaspoon nigella (black onion seeds)

1 teaspoon salt

2 teaspoons mustard oil or vegetable oil

1 garlic clove, finely chopped

¼ teaspoon cumin seeds

¼ teaspoon black mustard seeds

Warm Roti (see page 257), Naan (see page 257) or Grilled Flatbread (see page 131), to serve

Cook the eggplants over a gas flame or on the barbecue, turning regularly for 10 minutes or until the skins are blackened and charred. Put them in a colander over the sink to allow the bitter juices to drain away. When cool enough to handle, peel the eggplants and discard the skin.

Chop the flesh and put it in a bowl with the yoghurt, onion, chilli, coriander, nigella and salt. Combine well, then spread the dip over a serving dish.

Heat the mustard oil in a small frying pan over medium heat. Add the garlic, cumin seeds and mustard seeds and shake for 1–2 minutes until the seeds start to pop and the garlic turns golden. Remove from the heat and pour over the eggplant dip. Serve with warm roti, naan or flatbread.

GET AHEAD The dip can be made earlier in the day, then covered and refrigerated. Drain any excess water and stir well. Make the flavoured oil just before serving and pour over the top. Serve cold or gently reheat.

Serve this fresh chopped salad alongside grilled meat or scoop it up with poppadoms. The spices, as well as the lime dressing, give this a spicy sharp note and the peanuts add a salty crunch.

INDIAN-STYLE CUCUMBER SALAD
PREPARATION: 15 MINUTES • SERVES: 4–6 AS A SNACK

3 Lebanese (short) cucumbers or
  ½ telegraph (long) cucumber
1 red onion, finely chopped
3 roma (plum) tomatoes, seeded and
  diced
4 radishes, roughly chopped
small handful of coriander (cilantro)
  leaves, roughly chopped
1 each thumb-size red and green
  chilli, seeded and finely diced
juice of 1 lime
1 tablespoon vegetable oil
2 tablespoons chopped roasted
  salted peanuts
large pinch of mild chilli powder
½ teaspoon ground cumin
½ teaspoon chaat masala (optional)

Poppadoms, to serve

Peel the cucumbers, then cut them in half lengthways and remove the seeds with a teaspoon. Finely dice the cucumber flesh and put it in a bowl. Add all of the remaining ingredients including the chaat masala, if using, and toss to combine well. Serve with poppadoms.

GET AHEAD Chop the salad ingredients earlier in the day and keep them in separate bowls in the refrigerator. Toss together with the spices just before serving.

This curry is from Gujarat state, which has a predominantly vegetarian population. The tomato sauce, with flecks of coconut and spices, gets its zing from tamarind, a signature flavour in their cuisine. Midweek I do use ready-made curry pastes and spice mixtures such as garam masala, but this is one dish that especially benefits from freshly toasted and ground spices.

CAULIFLOWER & TOMATO CURRY

PREPARATION: 20 MINUTES • COOKING: 45 MINUTES • SERVES: 4–6

1 teaspoon coriander seeds

1 teaspoon cumin seeds

1 teaspoon fennel seeds

1 dried long red chilli (Kashmiri chilli, if available)

2 onions, 1 quartered, 1 thinly sliced

3 garlic cloves, chopped

5 cm (2 inch) piece ginger, peeled and sliced

2 thumb-size green chillies, 1 halved and seeded, 1 thinly sliced

1½ tablespoons vegetable oil

½ teaspoon ground turmeric

2 teaspoons black or yellow mustard seeds

400 ml (14 fl oz) tomato passata (puréed tomatoes)

50 g (1¾ oz) tamarind purée

250 ml (9 fl oz/1 cup) vegetable stock

2 tablespoons desiccated (shredded) coconut

1 cauliflower, about 500 g (1 lb 2 oz), cut into florets

Steamed rice, coriander (cilantro) leaves and Fresh Mango Chutney (see page 255), to serve

Put the coriander seeds, cumin seeds, fennel seeds and the dried chilli in a small frying pan and dry-fry, shaking, over medium heat for 40 seconds or until fragrant. Transfer the toasted spices to a spice grinder and process until fine.

Put the quartered onion, garlic, ginger and the halved green chilli in a blender or food processor and purée until smooth.

Heat the oil in a heavy-based saucepan over medium heat. Add the sliced onion and the puréed onion mixture and season well. Cook, stirring, for 10–12 minutes until golden. Add the ground spices, turmeric and mustard seeds and cook for another 2 minutes or until the mustard seeds begin to pop. Add the tomato passata, tamarind purée, stock and coconut and bring to the boil. Add the cauliflower, reduce heat to low, then simmer for 25 minutes or until the cauliflower is knife tender.

Serve the curry scattered with coriander leaves and the sliced green chilli, with steamed rice and Fresh Mango Chutney.

GET AHEAD You can make the curry base the day before but don't add the cauliflower. Cool the mixture, then cover and refrigerate. Gently reheat it in a saucepan and, when it is simmering, add the cauliflower and cook until tender, as above.

Hailing from Tamil Nadu in the south, this aromatic curry uses rarer Indian spices such as star anise and fennel seed in its mix. If you're passionate about Indian food you might want to pick up a coffee grinder, as roasting and grinding the spices is imperative. They are inexpensive and do a better job than a mortar and pestle.

CHETTINAD CHICKEN
PREPARATION: 20 MINUTES, PLUS 30 MINUTES MARINATING • COOKING: 45 MINUTES • SERVES: 4–6

3 large garlic cloves
2.5 cm (1 inch) piece ginger, peeled
  and coarsely chopped
750 g (1 lb 10 oz) boneless, skinless
  chicken thighs, cut into thirds
1 teaspoon ground turmeric
50 ml (1¾ fl oz) vegetable oil
1 large onion, sliced into thin
  half moons
1 thumb-size red chilli, seeded and
  sliced
1 tablespoon tomato paste
  (concentrated purée)
2 tablespoons desiccated (shredded)
  coconut
2 cinnamon sticks
350 ml (12 fl oz) vegetable stock

Steamed basmati rice and coriander
  (cilantro) leaves, to serve

Spice mix
1½ teaspoons fennel seeds
1½ teaspoons cumin seeds
1½ teaspoons coriander seeds
1½ teaspoons black peppercorns
1 star anise
1 dried long red chilli

To make the spice mix, combine all of the ingredients in a small frying pan and dry-fry, shaking the pan, over medium heat for 40 seconds or until fragrant. Cool slightly, then pour the toasted mixture into a spice grinder or mortar and pestle and finely grind.

Put the garlic, ginger and 1 tablespoon of water in a blender and process until smooth. Put the chicken thighs in a bowl, add the turmeric and then the garlic and ginger paste and season with salt and freshly ground black pepper. Cover and refrigerate for 30 minutes or overnight if time permits.

Heat the vegetable oil in a heavy-based saucepan over medium–high heat. Add the sliced onion and chilli and season with salt. Cook for 8–10 minutes or until soft. Add the chicken, ground spices, tomato paste, coconut and cinnamon sticks and cook for 5 minutes. Add the stock and simmer for 30 minutes or until the chicken is tender. Serve with steamed basmati rice and coriander leaves.

GET AHEAD The curry can be made in full the day before, then covered and refrigerated. Reheat gently in a covered saucepan until warm.

The Portuguese left their mark on Goan cuisine with the addition of vinegar in curries and pastes. Originally it was used as a substitute for wine, but it evolved to become a cornerstone of their cooking. Pork vindaloo is their most famous dish known for its fiery heat and it is adored by chilli afficionados around the world. Chunks of pork slowly simmer in aromatic sauce spiked with vinegar and spices such as cloves, cinnamon and cardamom until fork tender. This isn't too hot, so up the chilli if you like. Other meats, such as lamb neck or shoulder, would also work very nicely.

PORK VINDALOO

PREPARATION: 15 MINUTES, PLUS 4 HOURS MARINATING • COOKING: 2 HOURS • SERVES: 6–8

1.5 kg (3 lb 5 oz) pork shoulder
   or neck, trimmed of excess fat
50 ml (1¾ fl oz) vegetable oil
2 large onions, thinly sliced
2 garlic cloves, chopped
1½ teaspoons chilli powder
1½ teaspoons ground turmeric
2 cinnamon sticks
60 g (2¼ oz/¼ cup) tomato paste
   (concentrated purée)
50 ml (1¾ fl oz) malt or red wine
   vinegar

Steamed basmati rice and Red Onion
   Salad (see page 255), to serve

Marinade
5 Kashmiri or other dried long red
   chillies, seeded
½ cinnamon stick
2½ teaspoons cumin seeds
2½ teaspoons coriander seeds
6 cloves
6 black peppercorns
6 cardamom pods (seeds only)
5 cm (2 inch) piece ginger, peeled
4 garlic cloves
60 ml (2 fl oz/¼ cup) malt or red wine
   vinegar
1 teaspoon sugar
1 teaspoon salt

To make the marinade, put all of the spices in a small frying pan and dry-fry, shaking the pan, over medium heat for 40 seconds or until fragrant. Remove from the heat and cool slightly. Put the toasted spices in a spice grinder or mortar and pestle and finely grind, then transfer to a food processor. Add all of the remaining ingredients and process until smooth.

Cut the pork into 5 cm (2 inch) pieces and put it in a bowl. Add the marinade and toss to combine well. Cover and refrigerate for at least 4 hours, or overnight if time permits.

Drain the meat and season well with salt and freshly ground black pepper. Reserve the marinade.

Heat 1 tablespoon of vegetable oil in a large frying pan over high heat and cook the meat, in batches, for 2 minutes on each side or until golden. Remove from the pan and set aside. Reduce the heat to medium–low. Add the remaining oil, onion and garlic and stir for 10 minutes or until soft. Return the meat to the pan, add the reserved marinade, the spices, tomato paste, vinegar and 425 ml (15 fl oz) of water and combine well. Reduce the heat to as low as possible, cover and cook for 1–1½ hours or until the meat is very tender and falling apart. Check the seasoning and add extra vinegar, salt or sugar if necessary. Serve with steamed rice and Red Onion Salad.

GET AHEAD Marinate the meat up to 2 days ahead and make the curry in full 1 day ahead. Cover and refrigerate until serving and gently reheat in a covered saucepan.

SLOW OR FAST COOKING Cook the recipe in a slow cooker as a 4-hour short cook or cook it in 2 batches for 30 minutes each in a pressure cooker. Be sure to never fill the pressure cooker more than half full.

When in Goa a few years ago I fell in love with the grilled seafood on the beaches. Fresh fish, lobster and prawns were slathered with a chilli vinegar paste, barbecued and served with juicy limes. I was curious to find out the origin, as it didn't taste typically Indian. I later gleaned it was a legacy from the Portuguese, who occupied Goa for almost 400 years. It's a special paste called recheio masala that uses dried spices, chillies, garlic and vinegar and is used for marinades or as a curry base.

GRILLED SEAFOOD WITH GOAN MASALA PASTE
PREPARATION: 20 MINUTES • COOKING: 10 MINUTES • SERVES: 4

1 kg (2 lb 4 oz) mixed seafood, including raw prawns (shrimp) in the shells, halved raw lobster tails and deboned fish fillets with skin such as salmon, rainbow trout or redfish
2 tablespoons vegetable oil, for grilling

Lime wedges, coriander (cilantro) sprigs, chopped pineapple and Fresh Mango Chutney (see page 255), to serve

Recheio masala
6 Kashmiri or other long dried red chillies
60 ml (2 fl oz/¼ cup) boiling water
1 teaspoon cumin seeds
1 teaspoon ground turmeric
¼ teaspoon ground cloves
¼ teaspoon ground cinnamon
½ small onion
2 cm (¾ inch) piece ginger, peeled
5 garlic cloves
1 tablespoon tamarind purée
2 tablespoons malt vinegar
1 tablespoon sugar

To make the recheio masala, remove the stems and seeds from the chillies. Put them in a heatproof bowl and cover with the boiling water. Stand for 10 minutes, then transfer the chillies and water to a blender with all of the remaining ingredients and a good teaspoon of salt. Purée until smooth and set aside.

Using a pair of kitchen scissors, cut through the shell down the back of the unpeeled prawns and remove the vein. The shell will protect the prawns during cooking and the cut makes it easier for guests to pull the shells off. Spread a bit of the recheio masala on all of the seafood including the fish but not the prawn shells. Brush the shells with oil so they don't stick to the barbecue. If you like, you can thread the prawns onto metal skewers or wooden ones that have been soaked in water for 15 minutes to prevent them from burning during cooking.

Heat a barbecue, chargrill pan or grill (broiler) to high. Grill the seafood for 5 minutes or until the flesh is cooked. Bigger pieces may take longer. Serve with the lime wedges, coriander sprigs, chopped pineapple and the chutney.

GET AHEAD The recheio masala can be made up to 1 week ahead of time, covered and refrigerated. Prepare and clean your seafood earlier in the day and refrigerate until ready to cook. The ingredients for the Fresh Mango Chutney can be chopped earlier in the day but don't mix the ingredients together until just before serving.

Kati rolls are rotis or parathas that have a thin layer of egg fried on one side and are then filled and rolled with chicken, grilled beef and various chutneys and onions. Served at roadside stalls, these wondrous flatbread rolls are breakfast and lunch all in one. If you're not a fan of eggs, just wrap up chicken on its own.

SPICY CHICKEN KATI ROLLS

PREPARATION: 20 MINUTES • COOKING: 30 MINUTES • SERVES: 4–6

8 boneless, skinless chicken thighs

2 tablespoons vegetable oil,
   plus extra

1 large onion, halved and thinly sliced
   into half moons

2 garlic cloves, finely chopped

3 cm (1¼ inch) piece ginger, peeled
   and finely chopped

½ teaspoon ground cumin

½ teaspoon ground turmeric

½ teaspoon garam masala

1 tablespoon tomato paste
   (concentrated purée)

1 thumb-size red chilli, thinly sliced

1 tablespoon lemon juice

6 Roti (see page 257) or other
   flatbread

2 eggs, lightly beaten

Red Onion Salad (see page 255),
   store-bought lime pickle or mango
   chutney, and Mint, Green Chilli
   & Yoghurt Dipping Sauce (see
   page 254), to serve

Chop the chicken into bite-size pieces. Heat the vegetable oil in a large frying pan over low to medium heat. Add the onion, garlic, ginger and a pinch of salt. Cook for 10 minutes or until soft. Increase the heat to high. Add the chicken and cook for 5 minutes or until browned all over. Add the spices, tomato paste, chilli and lemon juice. Season well and cook for 10 minutes or until the chicken is tender. Remove from the heat and transfer to a serving bowl.

Heat a drizzle of extra oil in a clean frying pan over medium–high heat. Cook the roti, 1 at a time for 1 minute on one side. Turn and drizzle 1–2 tablespoons of the beaten egg over the top. Flip the roti back over and cook for another 30 seconds. Remove from the pan and spread the egg-covered side with the chicken, red onion salad, lime pickle or mango chutney and the mint, green chilli and yoghurt sauce. Fold up into a roll and serve with plenty of napkins.

GET AHEAD The chicken can be prepared in full the day before, then covered and refrigerated. Gently reheat to serve. Heat the roti with the egg just before serving.

Chana masala is a popular street food all over India. This fragrant vegetarian curry is perfect when you want a meat-free dinner. If you forget to soak the chickpeas overnight then simply cover with water and bring them to the boil with 3 teaspoons of bicarbonate of soda (baking soda), then turn off the heat, cover with a lid and stand for 1 hour. Drain, then boil as per the recipe. Tinned chickpeas are fine for a quick dinner, but chickpeas become more special if cooked from dried.

SWEET & SOUR CHICKPEAS
PREPARATION: 15 MINUTES, PLUS OVERNIGHT SOAKING • COOKING: 2 HOURS 15 MINUTES • SERVES: 4–6

400 g (14 oz) dried chickpeas, or three 400 g tins, drained and rinsed
50 ml (1¾ fl oz) vegetable oil
2 large onions, chopped
3 garlic cloves, chopped
4 cm (1½ inch) piece ginger, peeled and chopped
1 thumb-size green chilli, seeded and chopped
2½ tablespoons tomato paste (concentrated purée)
2 cinnamon sticks
1 teaspoon ground turmeric
2 teaspoons ground cumin
2 teaspoons coriander seeds
2 teaspoons garam masala
2 teaspoons chaat masala (optional)
juice of 2 lemons
100 g (3½ oz) green beans, trimmed and halved
1 large handful of coriander (cilantro) sprigs, chopped

Steamed basmati rice, Red Onion Salad (see page 255), Greek-style yoghurt and Fresh Mango Chutney (see page 255), to serve

If using dried chickpeas, put them in a large bowl, cover with cold water and soak overnight. Drain, then put them in a saucepan and add enough cold water to cover well. Bring to the boil, then simmer over medium heat for 1–1½ hours or until tender. Drain the chickpeas and reserve the cooking liquid.

Heat the oil in a large saucepan over medium high heat. Add the onion, garlic, ginger and chilli. Season with salt and freshly ground black pepper and cook for 10 minutes or until the onions are soft. Add the tomato paste, cinnamon sticks, turmeric, cumin, coriander seeds, half the garam masala and half the chaat masala, if using, and cook for 2–3 minutes. Add the chickpeas, lemon juice and 1 litre (35 fl oz/4 cups) of the chickpea cooking liquid. If using tinned chickpeas, then use vegetable stock or water. Simmer for 30 minutes or until the sauce is thick and flavourful.

About 5 minutes before the chickpeas are done, add the green beans, chopped coriander sprigs and the remaining garam masala and chaat masala, if using. Adjust the seasoning with extra lemon juice or salt if necessary. Serve with steamed basmati rice, Red Onion Salad, yoghurt and chutney.

GET AHEAD The curry can be made up to the point of adding the beans up to 2 days ahead, covered and refrigerated. Reheat gently and stir in the beans, coriander and remaining spices.

PRESSURE COOKER Instead of waiting an hour for the fresh chickpeas to cook, use your pressure cooker. Cook on high for 10 minutes and don't fill the pot more than half full.

The coconut-based curries of the south are lush with fresh seafood and chillies. They're the kind of dishes that linger in your mind after your travels. This one is very quick to make and puts an exotic dinner on the table in less than 20 minutes. Try the same creamy base with chicken or chunks of fresh fish for a light and easy meal.

COCONUT & TAMARIND SALMON CURRY WITH MUSTARD SEEDS

PREPARATION: 15 MINUTES • COOKING: 25 MINUTES • SERVES: 4

2 tablespoons desiccated
  (shredded) coconut
1½ tablespoons vegetable oil
1 large onion, halved and thinly sliced
  into half moons
2 garlic cloves, finely chopped
1 thumb-size green chilli, seeded
  and sliced
3 cm (1¼ inch) piece ginger, finely
  chopped
2 teaspoons ground cumin
2 teaspoons ground coriander
1 teaspoon ground turmeric
2 teaspoons black mustard seeds
100 g (3½ oz) tamarind purée
1 tablespoon tomato paste
  (concentrated purée)
400 ml (14 fl oz) tin coconut milk
500 g (1 lb 2 oz) skinless salmon fillet
  (pinbones removed), barramundi
  cod or halibut, cut into 6 cm
  (2½ inch) pieces
10 curry leaves (optional)

Steamed basmati rice and chopped
  coriander (cilantro) leaves, to serve

Preheat the oven to 160°C (315°F) or 140°C (275°F) fan forced. Spread the coconut on a baking tray and toast for 3–4 minutes or until the edges turn golden. Remove and transfer to a bowl.

Heat the vegetable oil in a large saucepan over medium–high heat. Add the onion, garlic, chilli and ginger and season with salt and freshly ground black pepper. Cook for 10 minutes or until golden and soft. Add the spices and cook for 1–2 minutes or until the mustard seeds pop. Add the tamarind purée, tomato paste, coconut milk, toasted coconut and 60 ml (2 fl oz/¼ cup) of water and simmer for 5 minutes or until slightly thickened.

Just before serving, add the salmon pieces and curry leaves, if using. Cook for 3–4 minutes or until just cooked to your liking. Serve with steamed basmati rice and chopped coriander.

GET AHEAD The base for the curry can be made the day before, then covered and refrigerated. Gently reheat before serving and add the fish when it comes to a simmer.

TAMARIND PURÉE

Be sure to buy the ready-to-go strained type of tamarind purée that is sold in jars and not the thick, unstrained paste. I find the Indian pastes slightly bitter, but the purées in jars are tart and fully diluted.

In the stifling heat of India, a lassi is a welcoming refreshment to cool yourself down. I've take the winning combination of subtle cardamom spice mixed with yoghurt and mango and fashioned it into a frozen treat. When making frozen iceblocks you normally need to add a simple sugar syrup: agave syrup makes a faster and healthier replacement and there is no need to wait for it to cool down before using it.

MANGO LASSI ICEBLOCKS

PREPARATION: 10 MINUTES, PLUS 4 HOURS FREEZING • MAKES: 8

4 very ripe mangoes, peeled, flesh
  roughly chopped: you will need
  about 400 g (14 oz) flesh
50 ml (1¾ fl oz) agave nectar
  or simple sugar syrup (see note)
250 g (9 oz) Greek-style yoghurt
¼ teaspoon ground cardamom

Put the chopped mango flesh in a blender or food processor and purée until smooth. Add the agave nectar and blend again.

Combine the yoghurt and cardamom in a bowl.

Pour 2 tablespoons of the mango puree into eight 100 ml (3½ fl oz) iceblock (popsicle/ice lolly) moulds. Spoon some yoghurt on top and repeat the layers until the moulds are filled. Add a wooden iceblock stick and freeze for at least 4 hours.

NOTE To make a simple sugar syrup, combine equal quantities of sugar and water in a saucepan and stir over low heat until the sugar dissolves. Bring to the boil, then remove from the heat and stand until cool.

GET AHEAD The iceblocks will keep frozen for up to 1 month.

EXTRAS & SIMPLE SIDES

DATE & TAMARIND DIPPING SAUCE
PREPARATION: 15 MINUTES • MAKES: 200 ML (7 FL OZ)

Soft medjool dates are the best kind to use for this dipping sauce. If you have dried dates, simply soak them in boiling water for 10 minutes, then drain.

4 soft dates, pitted and chopped
150 g (5½ oz) tamarind purée
1 teaspoon finely grated ginger
½ teaspoon ground cumin
½ teaspoon ground fennel
¼ teaspoon chilli powder
1½ tablespoons soft brown sugar

Combine all of the ingredients in a blender with 50 ml (1¾ fl oz) of water and a pinch of salt. Purée until smooth. Pour the mixture into a small saucepan and simmer for 10 minutes over medium heat, then leave to cool to room temperature.

GET AHEAD The sauce will keep for 1 week covered and stored in the refrigerator.

MINT, GREEN CHILLI & YOGHURT DIPPING SAUCE
PREPARATION: 5 MINUTES • MAKES: 250 ML (9 FL OZ/1 CUP)

Keep refrigerated in an airtight container for up to 3 days.

200 g (7 oz/¾ cup) Greek-style yoghurt
small handful of fresh mint leaves
small handful of coriander (cilantro) leaves
2 thumb-size green chillies, stems and seeds removed
1 red shallot, peeled
3 teaspoons caster (superfine) sugar

Combine all of the ingredients in a food processor with a large pinch of salt and purée until smooth. Pour into a bowl for serving.

FRESH MANGO CHUTNEY

PREPARATION: 10 MINUTES • MAKES: 250 ML (9 FL OZ/1 CUP)

Best served on the day of making.

1 mango, peeled and diced
½ green chilli, seeded and diced
½ small red onion, thinly sliced
juice of 1 lime
½ teaspoon ground cumin

Combine all the ingredients with a pinch of salt in a bowl.

CORIANDER CHUTNEY

PREPARATION: 5 MINUTES • MAKES: 125 ML (4½ FL OZ/½ CUP)

Best served on the day of making.

large handful of coriander (cilantro) leaves
  and stems, washed well
small handful of mint leaves
2 thumb-size green chillies, seeded, finely chopped
1 garlic clove, finely chopped
3 teaspoons finely chopped ginger
juice of ½ lemon

Finely chop the herbs, then combine them in a bowl with the remaining ingredients and a pinch of salt.

RED ONION SALAD

PREPARATION: 5 MINUTES • MAKES: 125 ML (4½ FL OZ/½ CUP)

Best served on the day of making.

1 red onion, halved and sliced into half moons
1 handful of mint leaves, chopped
juice of 1 lime
½ teaspoon chilli powder

Combine all of the ingredients with a pinch of salt.

NAAN

PREPARATION: 15 MINUTES, PLUS 2 HOURS PROVING TIME •
COOKING: 10 MINUTES • MAKES: 6

If you have an electric mixer with a dough hook, these naan don't take much effort to make. See photograph of naan opposite.

250 g (9 oz/1⅔ cups) plain (all-purpose) flour
½ teaspoon baking powder
2 teaspoons sugar
½ teaspoon nigella (black onion seeds)
  or cumin seeds
½ teaspoon salt
150 ml (5 fl oz) milk
1 egg, lightly beaten
1 teaspoon dried yeast
3 teaspoons vegetable oil, plus extra for brushing
100 g (3½ fl oz) Greek-style yoghurt

Sift the flour into a bowl with the baking powder, then stir in the sugar, nigella and salt. Make a well in the centre.

Put the milk in a small saucepan and stir over low heat until it reaches blood temperature.

In another bowl, combine the egg, yeast, oil and yoghurt, then stir in the warm milk. Pour the milk mixture into the well and start combining with the flour mixture until the dough comes together. Knead the dough on a lightly floured work surface for 8–10 minutes until smooth and elastic. You can also do this in the bowl of an electric mixer fitted with a dough hook. Put the dough into a lightly oiled bowl, cover with plastic wrap and stand in a warm place for 2 hours or until doubled in size. The time will vary depending on the temperature of your kitchen.

Preheat the grill (broiler) on high. Lightly oil two large baking trays. Divide the dough into 6 pieces. Use your hands to shape the dough into 6 ovals about 14 cm (5½ inches) long. Pull one side down to form a droplet shape. Lay the naan on the oiled trays. Keep one tray covered with a tea towel (dish towel) and put the other under the grill. Make sure you don't put it too close to the element or the naan will burn before they are cooked through. Grill for 2 minutes on each side, then repeat with the remaining tray.

ROTI OR PARATHA

PREPARATION: 20 MINUTES, PLUS 30 MINUTES RESTING •
COOKING: 15 MINUTES • MAKES: 6

Roti have thin layers of sweet butter rolled through them before they're pan-fried, making them the ultimate flatbread.

100 g (3½ oz/⅔ cup) wholemeal
  (whole-wheat) flour
100 g (3½ oz/⅔ cup) plain (all-purpose) flour
150 ml (5 fl oz) warm water
1 tablespoon melted butter or ghee, plus extra
  for brushing

Combine the flours and a good pinch of salt in a large bowl and make a well in the centre. Pour the water and vegetable oil into the middle. Using a large spoon, slowly combine the ingredients until the dough comes together. Turn out onto a work surface and knead for 5 minutes or until soft and smooth. You can also do this in the bowl of an electric mixer fitted with a dough hook. Put the dough in a lightly oiled bowl, cover with plastic wrap and stand for 30 minutes.

Divide the dough into 6 pieces. Roll out each one on a lightly floured surface into a 16 cm (6¼ inch) circle. Brush the tops with oil or ghee, then fold in half. Brush again, then fold into quarters. Roll out each one into a 25 cm (10 inch) round. Keep them in a stack covered with a clean tea towel (dish towel).

Heat a cast-iron pan or heavy-based frying pan over medium–high heat. Take 1 roti and shake off any excess flour. Brush one side with oil or ghee and pan-fry for 1 minute. Turn and cook the other side for another minute. Repeat with the others and keep them warm under a tea towel.

HOW TO
COOK LIKE A PRO
AT HOME

Replicating favourite foods from your travels or local restaurants may seem daunting, but not if you have a few tricks up your sleeve and some basic pieces of kit. Cooking is miles more satisfying and successful—as well as faster—if you have the right tools. Not all the tricks require a wallet-busting shopping trip; your refrigerator and barbecue hold more power than you might realise. These are my top tips for restaurant-quality cooking.

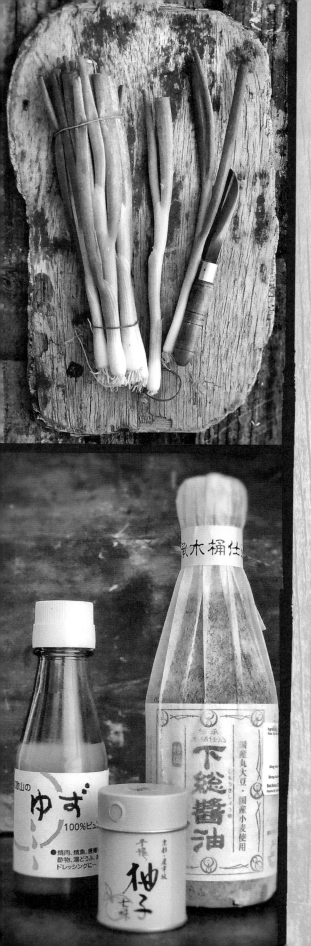

1 HIGH HEAT, LOW HEAT

Our mothers knew the value of pressure cookers to speed up cooking; luckily they don't look or sound as scary as they did in the fifties. Now they're more compact and easier to operate. If you love slow-cooked meat and freshly boiled legumes, then it's a no-brainer. Ribs and pulled pork take 20 minutes per batch versus 3 hours in a low-temperature oven. Never fill the pressure cooker more than half full and always cool under cold running water before opening the lid.

If you want to cook large batches of meat and forget about it, then a slow cooker is the ticket. Most come in large sizes and you can use either a 4- or 8-hour setting. A slow cooker is perfect for ribs, beef brisket, pulled pork or short ribs; they will cook up velvety soft with no tending needed.

2 CREATE THE WOOD-FIRED OVEN EFFECT WITH YOUR BARBECUE

Let's face it, smoke makes everything taste good. Barbecues not only impart that flavour, they also reach very high temperatures that ovens cannot. Most barbecues can heat up to 300°C (570°F), so pizzas and flatbreads cook quickly with the delicious aromas similar to a wood-fired oven. Once you get over any fear of the dough sticking (it doesn't) this will be an epiphany for you.

3 FILL THE PANTRY AND BE READY TO COOK

When a recipe calls for chipotle paste or pomegranate syrup, be ready. The street food featured in this book frequently requires unusual ingredients and it can be frustrating trying to find them on the day. Stock up on your vinegars, oils, pastes and spices so you're prepared to cook. Visiting your local Asian grocery or Mexican store is always an entertaining experience. Even if you don't have that luxury, nearly anything is available online these days.

4 THE POWER OF OVERNIGHT REFRIGERATION

Your refrigerator can do more than you think. It can slow down the rising of doughs for pizzas or flatbreads so you can barbecue or bake them when you're ready. Just bring them back to room temperature before you want to cook. The slow rising builds air pockets and more flavour so the crusts will be restaurant-style bubbly and chewy. Pasta and noodle dough can be left, covered, in the refrigerator for up to 2 days as well, so you're not constrained to make the noodles on the same day as kneading the dough. Store in a large resealable plastic bag and then bring the dough back to room temperature before rolling.

Brining and marinating meat or chicken is paramount for depth of flavour and tenderising. It takes some advance planning but it makes a huge difference to the taste and juiciness. If you marinate overnight in the refrigerator, that part of your prep is done and there is less to do on the day of cooking.

5 INVEST IN A STANDING ELECTRIC MIXER

Standing electric mixers can save you a lot of mess and aggravation. They are a large investment but most will last a lifetime. Babyskin-smooth dough for flatbreads, pizza or noodles can be made in 10 minutes with the dough hook attachment, versus 30 minutes by hand. Oil your hands to remove the dough and it slides right out. It will no longer be a herculean task to make pizza midweek and making dough will become part of your cooking repertoire.

Perfect crisp meringues, buttercream icings and cake batters are consistently better using an electric mixer fitted with the balloon whisk attachment. Although you can use an electric hand whisk, it doesn't have the motor power of an electric mixer.

6 USE A RICE COOKER

We're all guilty of buying kitchen gear that gets relegated to the appliance graveyard, gathering dust, but a rice cooker will never be one of those. Some rice, such as basmati, is very simple to cook but other varieties—such as Japanese medium-grain (sushi) rice or American long-grain—can be very tricky indeed. Rice cookers do all the hard work for you and are little pods of genius, keeping the rice perfectly warm for up to an hour without overcooking it.

The best and least expensive are the Japanese or Korean brands. A six-cup rice cooker is probably the biggest you will need (that amount makes up to 10 large rolls of sushi) and is fairly small in size. Avoid the posh digital versions (they're too hard to figure out and they're pricey) and buy one with a simple 'on' button, and you'll soon be the sensei of sushi making.

7 ROAST THE BONES BEFORE YOU MAKE STOCK

A good stock will make or break your Asian soups and noodle dishes and it's not an impossible task. Roasting the bones and vegetables before simmering is the secret. Years ago, I would boil my stock for hours only to find it tasted of dishwater. Roasting caramelises all the flavours and imparts a rich golden colour to the finished broth. Very low heat is vital: if the stock boils too hard it will be cloudy, and you want a clear liquid. Partially cover the stockpot with a lid to prevent it from evaporating. This works for any type of meat or even a pure vegetable stock. You will be amazed at the result.

8 FOOD WILL ONLY BE AS GOOD AS THE RAW INGREDIENTS

I know everyone tells you this but it is actually true. If your ingredients are amazing, they will sing in your cooking. Look for meat from farms that embrace free range and grass or grain feeding. There's a reason why Iberian pork tastes so unique and superior: it's the animal's controlled diet. The black pigs exclusively eat acorns, and the sweet nutty taste comes across in every bite. Corn-fed chicken flesh has a markedly yellow colour and superior flavour, so try to buy them when you can.

Farmers' markets or local greengrocers are treasure troves for inexpensive seasonal vegetables. If it hasn't been flown halfway around the world and not been long out of the ground, it's going to taste better. Bunches of baby beetroot (beets), artichokes and multicoloured tomatoes aren't likely to be in your supermarket, so these are the places to find special things.

9 USE BIG BAKING TRAYS AND FRYING PANS

Julia Child once said, 'The key to succesfully browning mushrooms is space.' If you overcrowd pans, they steam without browning. Food needs room to sear properly and it's essential to have a big heavy-based frying pan. Your dishes will cook faster with less chance of burning if the pan has a good thick base. Perfectly browned steaks and seared fish aren't achievable without a decent pan.

The same principle is true with baking trays. Your chips or roast veggies need that hot air swirling around them to crisp. Put too many on a small tray and they cook up soggy. Pick up some large heavy baking trays so everything can spread out and cook to golden perfection.

10 INVEST IN A DECENT-SIZE WOK

A big, good-quality wok doesn't cost much money and it will infinitely benefit your stir-frying. The principle of wok-frying is to quickly sear and stir-fry over very high heat. Overloading a small wok will make the ingredients soggy. Noodle dishes such as pad Thai need this type of space to succeed.

Forget about buying a deep-fryer and use your wok instead. The unique shape uses far less oil and keeps the temperature consistent. Deep-frying can ruin certain saucepans, so it's best to use your wok, which will also keep it well seasoned. Asian grocery stores are the best place to purchase one.

11 GET AHEAD: THINK LIKE A CHEF OR CATERER

Professionals would never be able to achieve their expert results without their *mise en place* (staging) of the cooking. Prepping ahead allows you to concentrate on what you're doing, make sure it tastes good and then clean the kitchen before anyone comes over.

Each recipe in this book tells you how to stage and what you can do ahead of time. Most foods can be prepared earlier in the day, then covered and stored in the refrigerator. The trick is to use baking paper under and over the food with plastic wrap over the top. The paper absorbs the moisture and the plastic wrap keeps it dry and protected. So if you're making gyoza, for instance, you can prepare them in the morning, wrap them up, and take them out of the refrigerator or freezer just before cooking. Enjoy the fruits of your efforts without being a frazzled, tired cook.

12 JULIENNE AND MANDOLIN TOOLS

Life is too short to julienne by hand, so buy a tool instead. Many Asian recipes call for the vegetables to be chopped this way—and you will zip through your prep faster if you are armed with one of these. Try out different models until you find the one that has the perfect thickness and size, as there are many variations.

Mandolins can be handy for thinly slicing onions and garlic, and you don't need to spend a bomb to have a good one. My favourite is the Japanese Kyocera ceramic handheld type. Amazon sells them very cheaply and they also make a julienne version. Both come with a little hand guard and stay sharp for a long time.

13 SHOW OFF YOUR FOOD

I work as a food stylist for London magazines as well as writing recipes and I couldn't be more emphatic about the importance of presentation. I'm not talking about dinnertime for the family, but if you're having friends around just think about a few basic things to make your food look as good as it tastes:

- display food on shallow platters, which make food look better than deep bowls;
- chop and add herbs close to serving so they stay green and fresh;
- serve dips on plates, spread out with extra virgin olive oil drizzled over;
- show off your food on white servingware, as colour competes;
- don't overcrowd the plate or platter;
- pick up stylish accents such as colourful chopsticks, serving spoons and dipping bowls;
- perk up the colour of brown food with fresh chopped herbs, sliced red chilli, a few cherry tomatoes or lemon and lime slices.

INDEX

ACKNOWLEDGMENTS

This book is dedicated to my three hungry boys: my husband, Patrick, and two sons, Liam and Riley. In the two years of creating, writing and testing the recipes in this book, you've washed towers of dishes, endured consecutive weeks of one cuisine, and have been the perfect arbiters of good taste.

My biggest thanks goes to Diana Hill. You believed in my idea, took a leap of faith and guided me to repackage my proposal so it became a reality. You're a true ambassador with people, very supportive, and I love your infectious laugh.

Miriam Steenhauer, you've worked so hard on the beautiful design for this book and I'm so glad we got to meet up in London. Thank you for being so calm during this whole process and not wanting to kill me when I asked for so many changes!

I was very fortunate to have the meticulous food-editing eye of Christine Osmond. You combed through my recipes as though they were your own and snapped everything beautifully into shape. International conversions are always challenging, but you made it easy. I wish the world would choose one measurement system!

Barbara McClenahan and Melody Lord, thank you for steering this ship to stay on course. I appreciate your patience when the editing came rather slowly from my side. Juggling freelance work and a book is always tricky, but we got there in the end. Everyone at Murdoch Books has been a pleasure to work with.

Jean Cazals, you are a mighty talented photographer. The photos we created for this book are sooo beautiful. Thank you for all your hard work, extra days and the priceless Chinese newspapers and antique Japanese chopsticks that endlessly popped out of your magical cupboards. You have a great eye for what works, tell good stories and always manage to find the pièce de résistance.

Emma Godwin, Sian Henley and Cat Byers: I owe a huge debt of gratitude for your expert prepping and hard work assisting in the kitchen. They were long days and space was tight. It was fun hanging out, talking and cooking. I can't tell you how much I appreciate the energy and enthusiasm you gave this.

I'm very grateful to Sarah Birks. Not only did you help me design my original proposal but also helped me start the prop styling. We've known each other a long time, at many magazines, and you are very generous at helping your friends.

A massive thanks to Jo Harris at Topham House for your extremely generous pricing for our props. So many of your exquisite bowls, plates and backgrounds graced our photographs. I'd also like to thank The Lacquer Chest for the treasures we rented: each of them is one of a kind. Emma Godwin, your beautiful and unique props were used in many chapters. Thank you for the amazing deal. Your distressed green table proved to be the killer background in many a photo.

Penny Subbiton, thank you for casting your expert eye on my bits of writing and listening to my weekly rants, doubts and worries about all sorts of things. You are a great friend in so many ways.

Published in 2015 by Murdoch Books, an imprint of Allen & Unwin
Reprinted 2017, 2018

Murdoch Books Australia
83 Alexander Street
Crows Nest NSW 2065
Phone: +61 (0) 2 8425 0100
Fax: +61 (0) 2 9906 2218
murdochbooks.com.au
info@murdochbooks.com.au

Murdoch Books UK
Ormond House
26–27 Boswell Street
London WC1N 3JZ
Phone: +44 (0) 20 8785 5995
murdochbooks.co.uk
info@murdochbooks.co.uk

For Corporate Orders & Custom Publishing, contact our Business Development
Team at salesenquiries@murdochbooks.com.au

Publisher: Diana Hill
Editorial Manager: Barbara McClenahan
Design Manager: Madeleine Kane
Project Editor: Melody Lord
Designer: Miriam Steenhauer
Photographer: Jean Cazals
Stylist: Jennifer Joyce
Food Editor: Christine Osmond
Production Manager: Mary Bjelobrk, Rachel Walsh

Text © Jennifer Joyce 2015
The moral rights of the author have been asserted.
Design © Murdoch Books 2015
Photography © Jean Cazals 2015

A cataloguing-in-publication entry is available from the catalogue of the
National Library of Australia at nla.gov.au.

ISBN 978 1 74336 418 5 Australia
ISBN 978 1 74336 459 8 UK

A catalogue record for this book is available from the British Library.

Colour reproduction by Splitting Image Colour Studio Pty Ltd,
Clayton, Victoria

Printed by C & C Offset Printing Co. Ltd., China

IMPORTANT: Those who might be at risk from the effects of salmonella poisoning
(the elderly, pregnant women, young children and those suffering from immune
deficiency diseases) should consult their doctor with any concerns about eating
raw eggs.

OVEN GUIDE: You may find cooking times vary depending on the oven you are
using. For fan-forced ovens, as a general rule, set the oven temperature to 20°C
(35°F) lower than indicated in the recipe.

MEASURES GUIDE: We have used 20 ml (4 teaspoon) tablespoon measures. If you
are using a 15 ml (3 teaspoon) tablespoon add an extra teaspoon of the ingredient
for each tablespoon specified.